Fire and Light:
The Saints and Theology

On Consulting the Saints, Mystics, and Martyrs in Theology

WILLIAM M. THOMPSON

PAULIST PRESS New York/Mahwah

Copyright © 1987 by
William M. Thompson

Library of Congress Cataloging-in-Publication Data

Thompson, William M.
    Fire and Light.

    Includes index.
        1. Theology—Methodology.   2. Christian saints.
3. Mysticism—Catholic Church.   4. Catholic Church—
Doctrines.   I. Title
BR118.T49   1987   235'.2   87-6918
ISBN 0-8091-2891-8 (pbk.)

Published by Paulist Press
997 Macarthur Boulevard
Mahwah, N.J. 07430

Printed and bound in the United States of America

Contents

FOR PATRICIA
still a very special fire and light

O my God . . . you have appeared as fire.
O you who are all love, O divine fire, you are completely
other, in your life, your ardor and your wide love, than what
we see in this element which warms our body. O my Jesus,
fire consumed in your Father, and consuming in yourself all
souls, have God, who appears to us in this fire and acts upon
our bodies physically, extend, if he wishes, his divine and
penetrating action into our souls.

Jean-Jacques Olier

Paul . . . saw absolutely no limit to his vision and to the light
which shone round about him; but rather it was as it were
a sun infinitely brighter and greater than the universe, with
himself standing in the midst of it, having become all eye.

St. Gregory Palamas

It is like approaching a fire; even though the fire may be a
large one, it will not be able to warm you well if you turn
away and hide your hands, though you may still get more
heat than you would if you were in a place without one.

St. Teresa of Avila

And then our good Lord opened my spiritual eye, and
showed me my soul in the midst of my heart. . . . I understood that it is a fine city.

And the greatest light and the brightest shining in the city
is the glorious love of our Lord God, as I see it.
Julian of Norwich

She then saw a ladder of flame and felt herself drawn up-
wards, experiencing great joy therein. This vision lasted for
about four hours.
St. Catherine of Genoa

Author's Preface

This work owes not a small amount to my devout Basque grandmother who almost daily kissed the feet of the statue of Our Lady of Lourdes in the bishop's chapel in Boise and encouraged me to do the same, by example and by exhortation. Those experiences of affection were certainly a form of "fire," but they were also "exposures to the light" which shaped my growing self-understanding. Thus began, I think, what has always been my fascination for the saints (and the mystics and martyrs) and for a wisdom nourished on their depth of experience. In the light of this, reflecting back upon it all now, it was rather to be expected that I would "consult" the saints in varying ways throughout my theological studies and writings. But I did this in a particularly sustained manner in my recent *The Jesus Debate* and was deeply impressed by the kind of "mystical" christology which I found: one that at times experientially exemplified the more common conciliar and "doctrinal" christology, but also one that seemed to develop and even occasionally "correct" that christology. The saints could be benefactors of theology, so I had suspected for some time, and so I had now learned in a more reflective way. The fire and light which the saints are and can be for us has penetrated and illuminated me so much, that I simply "had to" write this book, in deep thanksgiving and with the hope that I might align myself with those other scholars and theologians who have also known something of the explosive power of the saints and desired to share this most remarkable gift with their colleagues.

1

Readers may have a tendency to think that "fire" modifies "saints" and "light," "theology." And, naturally, that makes a certain amount of sense. After all, the saints are "burning" with the love of God, are they not? It seems quite right, then, to think of the saints as particularly representative of love, affectivity, warmth, intuition, experience, praxis, and other similar realities. Theology, on the other hand, usually makes us think of theory, reason, illumination, etc. But the intent of this book is to help us overcome that rather too simple dichotomy. "Fire and light" is meant to modify both "saints" and "theology." The saints, precisely because of the searing depth of their lived experience, can be rich sources for a theology which wants to root itself in experience itself. And theology, precisely when it works from the fires of experience, seems to do its assigned work of lighting up our human experience best. Both the saints and theology seem to be a blend, in varying intensities, of fire and light. Precisely for that reason they should be attractive to one another and seek each other out. Any number of thinkers through the ages have noticed this and, at times, reflected upon it. Furthering this reflection upon the exchange or *perichoresis* that should and can exist between theology and sanctity is the major objective of this study.

I owe many thanks to my wife and children, to my other friends, and to my colleagues. "Behind every saint stands another saint," Von Hügel reminded us. This has certainly been confirmed by my experience over and over again. I gladly and thankfully acknowledge it. Here, however, the word "saint" is being used rather widely! But let me especially thank my wife Patricia Marie, to whom I dedicate this book. Over the years she has been, more than anyone else under God, at times more fire than light; at other times, more light than fire. And I have truly needed both!

Introduction

This "essay" is primarily intended to be a modest contribution toward our understanding and practice of the discipline of theology. It is a "hermeneutical" study, in other words, in the sense that theology is the art of interpreting and appropriating Christian experiences and Christian texts. The essay hopes to show that the experiences and texts of the saints, mystics, and martyrs ought normally to be consulted when theologians go about their work of mediating the Christian tradition to their contemporary situation. The saints are sources of theology, and even of doctrine. In line with this, my use of the word "consult" is meant to call to mind Cardinal Newman's great study *On Consulting the Faithful in Matters of Doctrine*. Just as that work opened up, and tried to rehabilitate the case for, the tradition of the "faithful laity" as sources of doctrine, so this essay would like to explore the case for the traditional view that the saints, the mystics, and the martyrs are similarly sources of theology and doctrine. Indeed, some would say that they are the privileged sources of the theologian. Paraphrasing St. Ignatius Loyola, we might suggest that *sentire cum sanctis et mysticis* ("attunement to the saints and mystics") could serve as a shorthand expression for this study's hermeneutical thrust.[1]

Before moving any further, some preliminary clarifications are in order. First, I do not intend to tackle some issues that commonly come up when the subject of saints arises: namely, the legitimacy of canonization by churches, the kinds of criteria to be used in determining canonizable saints,

3

and sociopolitical factors that seem to play a role in current canonization procedures. Secondly, we will assume the fact of the holy person or saint, a reality which seems to be a universal phenomenon. For our purposes, Lawrence Cunningham's definition provides us with a workable guide: "A saint is a person so grasped by a religious vision that it becomes central to his or her life in a way that radically changes the person and leads others to glimpse the value of that vision."[2] Perhaps we should add that the saint is someone grasped by both a religious vision *and praxis,* in order to bring out the practical, and even sociopolitical dimensions of sanctity. Saints not only adhere to a vision, but they in varying ways embody that vision quite practically in ecclesial and other social circumstances. I think, however, that this "praxis" dimension is at least implied in Cunningham's definition when it speaks of the transformation of life which the saint undergoes.

We might observe that this definition does not limit sanctity to the canonized, or officially recognized, saint. There are many who are profoundly transformed by the Christian vision and way of life, and whose lives intersect with others in an explosively transforming manner, and yet they do not achieve an "official" ecclesial recognition. So we can plausibly hold that sanctity can't be limited to *canonized* sanctity. Even so, this definition does not cheapen sanctity. Not every Christian is a saint, but only the transformed one. This is what the New Testament seems to mean when it speaks of the saints or holy ones: they are those who are *faithful* to the Lord (2 Cor 1:1; Eph 1:1; Phil 1:1; Col 1:2). Closer to our own time, St. Thérèse of Lisieux captured something of the depth of the saint's experience when she said,

> I have always noticed that when I compared myself to the saints, there is between them and me

> the same difference that exists between a moun-
> tain whose summit is lost in the clouds and the
> obscure grain of sand trampled underfoot by the
> passers-by.[3]

Thérèse exaggerates the "smallness" of the non-saint, but something of the explosiveness of the saint does reach us in her description. And we do seem to need a fair dose of the kind of humility she displays to be able to recognize the saint that appears before us.

I would also suggest that, for our purposes, martyrs and mystics should be considered together with the saints as composing one broad category. The tradition seems to consider the martyrs to be the saints *par excellence,* owing to the total gift of life they have made for and to God. The "non-sainted" and "non-martyred" mystics might plausibly be considered saints too, at least in the sense we're giving to the term "saint." Some might take exception to this equalizing of the saints and mystics, regarding the latter as people who manifest such extraordinary phenomena as ligatures, special revelatory visions and auditions, levitations, stigmata, and other similar things. But as I understand it, such phenomena do not seem to characterize all the noted mystics of history, and most contemporary scholars tend to consider such phenomena "accidental" rather than "essential" to the mystic state.

I also mentioned that this essay will be a somewhat "modest" one. By that I mean that I am not so much trying to break new ground as I am trying reflectively to report upon a theological strategy which possesses an extraordinary historical pedigree and seems to be enjoying an increasingly prominent rehabilitation among many of today's noted theologians. We will explore the "earlier" tradition a bit later in this book. For now, let us take a look at the contemporary situation.

To some extent the appeal to the saints in theological writing seems to represent something of a *novum*, a "novelty," at least when it's measured against the relatively recent past. Roman Catholic scholars of the post-Reformation and Baroque variety tended to consult the episcopal and papal magisterium as theology's key source. This came to be known as a "Denzinger" style of theology, after the name of the theologian who edited magisterial decrees into a handy volume. After the Second Vatican Council, Catholic theologians started to move away from this Denzinger-oriented style of theology toward a more biblically-oriented kind in large numbers. Protestant theologians, of course, possessed grave suspicions of the canonized saints (the reader will recall all the issues associated with relics, indulgences, etc.), and in any case have usually tended toward a more biblically-oriented style of theology. Even the Eastern Orthodox have endured a kind of dry, narrowly scholastic form of theology until the relatively recent renaissance among them of their rich patristic and mystic sources of theology. We should say, however, that the consultation of the saints by theologians always seemed to remain a more respected, if at times muted, theological strategy for the Orthodox than for the other ecclesial traditions.[4]

Why is there a renewed interest in theological consultation of the saints? Why do so many think that the biblical foundations of theology could usefully be complemented and perhaps even enriched by a probing of the experiences and writings of the saints? How widespread is this kind of "consultation" among the theologians of all the major ecclesial traditions? Is this new attunement to the saints and mystics a kind of nostalgia for a past form of Christianity, or does it represent a genuine revitalization of the faith for today? These are a few of the more basic questions this book hopes to explore with the reader.

Might I recommend, too, that as the reader approaches this study of the saints, attention should be paid to the great literary and artistic masters? I am thinking of those among them who have "pondered" and "expressed" the depths of the mystery of sanctity: El Greco, Bernini, Bernanos, Greene, Kazantzakis, Dostoyevsky, Solzhenitsyn, Mauriac, even Dante, etc. One surely finds among these a surfacing and exploration of our theme equal in content to any theological study. Often the powerful mixture of fire and light which the saints can be finds its "connatural" expression in the rather more aesthetic sphere. The theologian interested in sanctity ought to regard these great artists and writers as crucial companions on the way to a deeper appropriation of what the saints can mean for a revitalized theology.

Notes

[1]Cf. St. Ignatius Loyola, "Rules for Thinking with the Church," *The Spiritual Exercises of St. Ignatius*, Anthony Mottola, transl. (Garden City, N.Y.: Doubleday Image, 1964), pp. 139–142. Ignatius spoke of *sentire cum ecclesia*.

[2]Lawrence C. Cunningham, *The Meaning of Saints* (San Francisco: Harper and Row, 1980), p. 65, probably the best entry into the overall subject of sanctity. Some other helpful studies: Peter Brown, *The Cult of the Saints: Its Rise and Function in Latin Christianity* (Chicago: University of Chicago, 1981); Stephen Wilson, ed., *Saints and Their Cult: Studies in Religious Sociology, Folklore and History* (Cambridge: University Press, 1983); Donald Weinstein and Rudolph M. Bell, *Saints and Society: The Two Worlds of Western Christendom, 1000–1700* (Chicago: University of Chicago, 1982); Sergei Hackel, ed., *The Byzantine Saint: University of Birmingham Fourteenth Spring Symposium of Byzantine Studies*, *Sobornost* Supplement 5, Special No. of *Sobornost Incorporating Eastern Churches Review* (London: Fellowship of St.

Alban and St. Sergius, 1981); and Romano Guardini, *The Saints in Daily Christian Life* (Philadelphia: Chilton Books/Wilkes-Barre: Dimension Books, 1966).

[3]St. Thérèse of Lisieux, *Story of a Soul: The Autobiography of St. Thérèse of Lisieux* (Washington, D.C.: Institute of Carmelite Studies, 1975), p. 207.

[4]Cf. George A. Maloney, *A History of Orthodox Theology Since 1453* (Belmont, Maine: Nordland, 1976).

I

Today's Theologians and the Saints: An Overview

This chapter will not be a "sociological" study of how many contemporary theologians are actually consulting the saints as they go about their work. But it will primarily refer to theologians who are somewhat widely recognized, and I believe it will make the case for the view that there is something like a rehabilitation of the consultation of the saints among today's theologians. Throughout this book, of course, I am mainly limiting the discussion to the consultation of the *saints*. But if one were to add to this the program of overcoming a highly rationalistic, almost cerebral style of theology by somehow relinking theology and spirituality, theology and faith, theology and commitment, etc., then I think we could make an even stronger case for the consultation of the kinds of concerns represented by the saints among today's religious scholars. I will try to stay with my narrower focus of the consultation of the saints themselves. Still, I hope the reader will see the connection between this more limited perspective and the wider concerns that seem to be surfacing today. I'll try to explore some of this in a later chapter.

For now, let us attempt a sketch of the theological consultation of the saints, the mystics, and the martyrs. I'll move through the major subdisciplines of theology as it is practiced today: fundamental, systematic, and practical theology.

Fundamental Theology

In fundamental theology, for example, Yves Congar
notes that "modern treatises on theological criteriology give
a place to the acts of the martyrs and to the writings of the
saints." Congar's great book on tradition views the saints of
past and present as "privileged" and "spontaneous" monu-
ments of the tradition: "The Church lives above all in the
saints, and by the saints as well. They carry the Tradition
with a superior authority. . . ."[1] Karl Rahner's breakthrough
study of discernment in St. Ignatius Loyola argues that the
saints are too infrequently consulted as sources of theological
thought. At times they do not simply imitate the magisterial
theology, but become a "creative prototype" or an "original
assimilation" of divine revelation, and in this sense they are
one of theology's "sources."[2] Hans Urs von Balthasar emphatically and repeatedly—some might be tempted to say
"vehemently"—appeals to the saints as a privileged and perhaps even as the final source of theological speculation. In
a study of St. Thérèse of Lisieux he had early on suggested

> . . . that few things are so likely to vitalize and
> rejuvenate theology, and therefore the whole of
> Christian life, as a blood-transfusion from hagiog-
> raphy. Yet this must be done as a work of theol-
> ogy; the essence of sanctity has to be grasped as
> truly evangelical, as belonging to the Church, as
> a mission and not simply as an individual asceti-
> cal, mystical manifestation.

He suggests that "No one is so much himself as the saint,
who disposes himself to God's plan, for which he is prepared
to surrender his whole being, body, soul and spirit." God
seems to single out from the community of saints "special,
representative saints" for the good of the Church. "They are
irrefutable, beyond questioning, as indivisible as prime num-

bers." True theology is "the theology of the saints," says von Balthasar.[3]

Bernard Häring is a fine example of a Catholic moral theologian who has consistently integrated the appeal to the saints into his fundamental and special moral theology. His earlier *The Law of Christ* spoke of the "apostolate of good example," drawing attention to the importance of models for communicating moral teaching. He called the saints "moral geniuses" in this respect. His more recent work speaks more colorfully of the "magisterium of the saints," thus focusing the saints as a properly moral theological source.[4]

The appeal to the saints has usually formed a significant part of Eastern Orthodox fundamental theology. Latin theology's separation of theology and sanctity is seen by theologian-bishop Timothy Kallistos Ware as one of the sources of the schism. He illustrates what he would regard as the typically Eastern Orthodox mode of theologizing through Serbian bishop Nikolai Velimirovich's observations during a discussion of the sacraments at the 1927 Faith and Order conference in Lausanne:

> All that we have said about the great Christian
> Mysteries is not an opinion of our own . . . but it
> is the repeated experience of the Apostles in the
> ancient days and of the saints up to our own
> days. For the Church of God lives not on opin-
> ion, but on the experience of the saints, as in the
> beginning so in our days. The opinions of intel-
> lectual persons may be wonderfully clever and
> yet be false, whereas the experience of the saints
> is always true. It is God the Lord who is true to
> himself in his saints.

And Kallistos Ware adds his own gloss to this: while this may seem "an emotional and sentimental way of arguing" to the

western scholastic, to the Orthodox "it is precisely the experience of the saints that constitutes the final criterion in
theology."[5]

The theology stemming from the Reformation typically
takes a cautious posture toward the saints, as is well known.
But even here there are the "stirrings" of an appeal to the
saints as an important element of fundamental theology, provided one construes sanctity in the broad categories of this
essay. Robert Neville has contributed a phenomenological
study of the saint as a recurring manifestation of the religious
spirit. Geoffrey Wainwright's magisterial liturgical systematics views the experience of the saints as basic sources of
both liturgy and theology. Patrick Sherry has written an important study in which he attempts to ground a Christian
anthropology and eschatology at least partly on the lives and
writings of the saints. He sees validity to the argument that
the saints both model forth and reveal the nature and destiny
of all of us. The Anglican Michael Perham has probably written the most extensive monograph on the saints from a primarily Reformation perspective. He attempts a rather impressive rehabilitation of the category of the communion of
saints, citing important texts from the Reformers themselves.
He says, for example, that Luther praised the evangelical
martyrs of the Netherlands as "real saints." Calvin, he notes,
was more interested in the general category of sanctification,
rather than individual saints: ". . . Christ . . . justifies no
one whom he does not also sanctify." From the viewpoint of
fundamental theology, Perham considers the saints to be
"witnesses" to the Christ event, linking us with it down
through the ages of the tradition, and showing us how that
event can break through in ever new ways in the present
and future.[6]

Modern fundamental moral theology from a primarily
Protestant perspective does not disappoint us either. The

argumentum ex sanctis et mysticis occurs at least in the writings of the highly respected James Gustafson, for example. He has repeatedly argued that good moral discernment flows from a life steeped in the "piety" and prayer life of the tradition. I take this to be a more "reformed" way of speaking about spirituality and sanctity. Gustafson's point links up with the new stress upon an ethics of character: the moral life, at least in part, is a function of the formed personal character of the moral agent, which itself is co-constituted by the character-forming power of the Church and its tradition. In one of his essays Gustafson points to Mother Teresa of Calcutta as a paradigm of the kind of fusion between spirituality and morality that fosters authentic moral discernment.[7]

Speculative Theology (Systematics)

Virtually all the great themes of systematics have their representative thinkers who employ some form of the "appeal to the saints" in their writings. In this sense, they put the above fundamental theology to work, prolonging it in systematics. In some cases the saints seem to function as illustrations and confirmations of some facet of the Christian tradition as commonly understood. At other times and somewhat more daringly the appeal to the saints functions as a corrective to the tradition's dominant self-understanding, highlighting what seems understressed or disclosing what has been ignored. Both of these "uses" of the saints is noticeable among the authors from fundamental whom we have surveyed: Von Balthasar seems to stress the "confirmatory" function of appealing to the saints; the others, both functions. Rahner particularly stresses the corrective function in his remarkable study of Loyola's spiritual theology of discernment.[8]

Studies in the theology of revelation are a particularly

important example of the use of the saints and mystics in systematics, since the living response in faith to divine revelation as embodied in the saints provides a rather powerful example of the dynamics of the revelatory experience. Revelation and faith are issues hotly debated since the Enlightenment, and the appeal to the saints seems to provide the theologian with an "experiential" answer for an "experience-oriented," post-Enlightenment culture. The work of Baron Friedrich von Hügel is something of a paradigm here: he developed a phenomenology of the mystical experience to ground, experientially, the possibility and meaningfulness of a personal, revealing God. "Philosophies," he tells us, "that leave no room for prayer, adoration, sin, forgiveness, redemption, may be excellent in many other directions, and also as criticisms and stimulants of religious thought; but as would-be adequate theories of religion, they cannot fail more or less to misconceive and to explain away facts of inexhaustible vitality."[9] The appeal to the saints, in other words, provided Von Hügel with examples of a widened human experience which includes the religious dimension in an atmosphere which tended to reduce reality to sense experience alone. Other significant writers in this area have looked to the saints and mystics for similar purposes: Karl Rahner, Avery Dulles, David Tracy, Louis Dupré, Vladimir Lossky, Timothy Kallistos Ware, Eric Voegelin, Paul Tillich, Peter Berger, to mention only some representative thinkers. Von Hügel, John Macquarrie, and John Meyendorff have even consulted the mystics in an effort to elaborate a trinitarian theology of God. God as triune or tripersonal is frequently an insight learned by the mystic in her or his personal encounter with God.[10]

Students of Karl Rahner have long pointed out how his rich theological anthropology is to a great extent an extrapolation from the mystical experience of St. Ignatius Loyola,

St. Bonaventure, the Spanish mystics, even to some extent Cardinal Pierre de Bérulle. *Humanum* as *capax Infiniti* or hearer of the Word translates the Ignatian "openness to God as ever greater" and the Bonaventurian "itinerary of the soul to God." The influence of St. Teresa of Avila and Bérulle has aided Rahner in adding a christological twist to his anthropology: the human journey to the Divine is always a mediated journey, primarily through Jesus, but also through other holy mediators. [11]

Others, besides Rahner, have not been lacking who would apply the insights of the saints and mystics to the refurbishing of a theological anthropology. Clearly the border between revelation theology and anthropology, as they are practiced today, is fluid, and writers in the former category could plausibly be said to be contributors to theological anthropology too. But there are others who deserve a special mention here. For example, let us take the case of Von Balthasar. Like Rahner, he reads the Scriptures at least partly through the lens and spiritual exegesis of the *patres*, together with the mystics. And so it is hard to differentiate the varied influences in his thought. Is his anthropology biblical or mystical? For him that question would make no sense, for it presupposes a false dichotomy. Notice the fusion of Bible and mysticism in this citation, parallels of which could be heaped one upon the other: " . . . the great contemplatives are but realising in themselves the movement of all history, which bears witness to Christ merely by dying to itself and tending towards a form which transcends it."[12] This is a paschal anthropology which Von Balthasar thinks was supremely disclosed in Jesus and less powerfully in his sainted disciples. Let me end with one further anthropologist, this time from the Orthodox tradition. John Meyendorff, for example, suggests that Orthodox anthropology views "man as an 'open being,' naturally possessing in himself a divine 'spark' and

dynamically oriented toward further progress in God." This
is a "participationist" view of humanity as radically oriented
toward the Divine, and Meyendorff appeals to the Byzantine
theology of "participation in God" through deification as lived
by the saints as his theological foundation.[13]

Some have even viewed the martyrs, saints, and mystics
as important sources for a renewed christology and soteriology. This is perhaps somewhat more daring: one usually reasons from Jesus to the saints: the former is the paradigm;
the latter, the imitators. But authors see an analogous relationship between them, and so it should be possible as well
as plausible to note similarities between them. This is particularly helpful, since we possess no real "biography" of Jesus. Here again Rahner and Von Balthasar were pioneers.
One can easily note the application of Rahner's mystical anthropology to Jesus in this oft-cited statement: "The incarnation of God is therefore the unique, *supreme,* case of the
total actualization of human reality, which consists of the fact
that man *is* in so far as he gives up himself."[14] Von Balthasar
early on had suggested that we might learn a great deal about
Jesus' passion from the mystics' dark night:

> But it is the Church's teaching on the second
> Person, christology, that stands to gain from what
> the saints experienced. In fact, however, christol-
> ogy also has remained practically static within the
> formal setting of Chalcedon; its further growth as
> a result of the total experience of the Church's
> faith is still awaited. We can see this if we con-
> sider the state of what might be called passiology
> (why have we no word for it?). . . . The New
> Testament gives us very little that can serve to
> introduce us to the mysterious inner world of the
> passion. There is, however, more in the Old Tes-

tament, but it has never been made sufficient use of. Above all, there are the graces of participation in the passion given to the Church, the experiences of the saints, which are quite inexplicable except as a participation in Christ's states. These experiences constitute the vast, limitless field of the "dark nights," which, as described by those who underwent them, are so strikingly similar and yet offer such a variety of individual aspects. To my knowledge, no theology has seriously undertaken the task of seeing them as a whole and evaluating them from the point of view of dogma.[15]

It is well known that another significant christologian, Wolfhart Pannenberg, developed a relational anthropology much like Rahner's as a model for the hypostatic union, and he was in part dependent upon the rich mystical theology of the Victorines at this point, as he indicated.[16] The Orthodox, of course, view Jesus as the perfect human, most fully deified, because he most fully participates in the Divine. One can easily glimpse the accents of Byzantine mystical theology throughout the Orthodox christology.[17] In my own christological work, I have tried to probe the potential fruitfulness of the mystical experience as an experiential bridge to the Jesus event. The anthropology lived out by them seems to find its intensive manifestation in Jesus. Before reading Von Balthasar on this point, I had explored the dark night's implications for passiology and for the disclosure of God in the Jesus event. The martyrs, mystics, and saints are also, so I've found, something of a corrective to the predominant conciliar christology, resurfacing the image of Jesus as a humiliated Savior especially come for the suffering and oppressed. Jesus, in other words, is indeed a "relational person," but his network of relationships are not simply personal and interpersonal (with family and intimates), but social, political, and conflictual (with the powers of his day on behalf of the marginal). Studying Jesus through a "mystical exegesis" has aided me in surfacing this limitation of the conciliar-influenced christologies.[18]

Ecclesiology remains, to a great extent, largely unexplored from the point of view of our theme. Yet even here some pioneer work has been done, at least on a few ecclesial themes. It is well known that Eastern Orthodoxy often grounds its ecclesiology in the belief in the communion of saints. This communion is the lived experience of the saints, who transcend their own egoism in the service of a communitarian love which builds community. The Church flows from the common experience of sanctity, in other words. Of course, this is a theme dear to the churches of the Reformation too. In fact, traditionally the Reformed churches are much more comfortable speaking of sanctity in the plural (= the sanctified of the Church) than in the singular (the individual saints celebrated in Roman Catholicism and Orthodoxy). Peter Chirico, among Roman Catholics, has helpfully explored how ecclesiological themes might flow from the doctrine of the communion of saints. For Chirico, the risen Jesus is a kind of model of perfected humanity for the individual, while the communion of saints is a model for persons-in-community, ecclesially or extra-ecclesially.[19]

Less commonly, but still quite promisingly, some other ecclesial themes are being explored through a "mystical lens." Significant here, I think, is Harvey Egan's recent work on mysticism, in which he continually consults a number of important mystics for their theological teaching. He has an ecclesiological sensitivity which enables him to surface some of the potential ecclesial wealth of the mystics. He notes, for example, that St. Teresa of Avila, St. Ignatius Loyola, and

the author of *The Cloud of Unknowing* "lived the paradox
that genuine Christian mystics have always lived: an authentic willingness to measure their mystical interiority against
the norms of Church authority along with a will of steel,
ready to overcome any and all obstacles to what they perceived as God's will." Mystical experience is an ecclesial experience, in other words. At the same time, Egan underscores a kind of critical sensitivity in the ecclesial consciousness of some of the mystics. As Von Balthasar finds
christological insights in the dark night, Egan suggests that
we might find ecclesiological insights too. For example,

> In the spirituality and mysticism of St. John of
> the Cross, there is a tension between subjective
> experience and its objectifications in Church,
> scripture, and tradition, but there is never an op-
> position. The third stanza of *The Dark Night* does
> suggest that John took "no other light or guide
> than one that burned in my heart." On the other
> hand, he insisted that "we must be guided hu-
> manly and visibly in all by the law of Christ the
> man and that of His Church and of His minis-
> ters." . . . Contact with God, therefore, in no
> way removes the authentic mystic from Church
> and scripture. On the other hand, the night of
> faith through which mystics pass purifies and
> transforms their appreciation for and participation
> in scripture and Church. In fact, both scripture
> and Church are demythologized, purified, healed,
> and transformed along with the mystic.[20]

An ecclesial dark night symbolizes a Church *semper refor-
manda*, in other words.

Finally, eschatology has long been a privileged locus of
the appeal to the saints and mystics. Dante's *trivium* of the

inferno, purgatorio, and *paradiso* is surely an extrapolation from the mystical *via purgativia, illuminativa,* and *unitiva.* From the depths of one's own mystical experience, one perhaps finds clues or signs as to the future, "ultimate" destiny of humanity. This was Karl Rahner's way: " . . . we know no more about the last things than we know about people who have been redeemed, who have been taken up by Christ, and who exist in God's grace." Hence his famous suggestion that heaven and hell cannot be on an equal level: canonization teaches us that salvation is a reality; damnation would only seem to be a possibility.[21] The existence of the saint is, if you will, a living sign of "heaven" as the abode of salvation. The sufferings of the mystics are also commonly taken to be signs of what the symbol of purgatory points to. For example, St. Teresa of Avila says of her own mystical sufferings that "in this pain the soul is purified and fashioned or purged like gold in the crucible so that the enameled gifts might be placed there in a better way, and in this prayer it is purged of what otherwise it would have to be purged of in purgatory."[22] Somewhat more daringly, Von Balthasar has proposed that the special charism of the mystic Adrienne von Speyr is to light up "the mysteries of Holy Saturday and hence of hell and of universal redemption as well." Von Speyr's "experiences" of hell have convinced her of Jesus' descent to the realm of the dead: the divine compassion reaches even there. And Von Balthasar interestingly muses: "Has perhaps our time been made ready for this grace by the fact that the modern experience of the remoteness of God, of 'God is dead,' and even of the hellish dregs of human existence had to be undergone first before something like the charism of Adrienne von Speyr would be meaningful."[23]

Although all of the above eschatologists are Roman Catholics, still we can point to similar lines of inquiry within the other confessions. John Hick is well known for his use

of the Christian mystic's unitive state as at least a partial basis
for belief in heaven. "Thus in christian mysticism there is
something analogous to the widespread eastern conviction
that our approach to Ultimate Reality involves the transcending of ego-hood," Hick says.[24] And Vladimir Lossky can be
considered representative of the East when he tells us that
the Taboric light of full perfection in which we can participate in eternity is partially glimpsed in the saint's experience: "Mystical experience implies this change in our nature,
its transformation by grace." " . . . the entering into eternal
life . . . is being fulfilled here and now . . . before death and
the resurrection, in the saints who live in uninterrupted
communion with God." Additionally, I would suggest that
the Eastern Orthodox have particularly kept in focus what
Lossky calls "the Feast of the Kingdom," the collective belief
in the communion of saints spoken of earlier. This, too, is
an extrapolation from the lived experience of the saints and
mystics who dwell in selfless unity and mutual compassion
even now. This symbol of the communion of saints nicely
shows how collective or universal eschatology is somehow
linked to and grounded in the experience of the saints even
now.[25]

A particularly fascinating area deserving much more
thought is the mystical experience of death, which might
provide us with a corrective to the all too common agonizing
dread of death in our culture. In any case, Harvey Egan has
noted how John of the Cross "makes the fascinating observation that mortal life is not really snatched away from such
highly purified and transformed persons. They die gently
and sweetly in an ecstasy of love." In John's words:

>   . . . the death of persons who have reached this
>   state is far different in its cause and mode than
>   the death of others, even though it is similar in

natural circumstances. If the death of other people is caused by sickness or old age, the death of
these persons is not so induced . . . their soul is
not wrested from them unless by some impetus
and encounter of love, far more sublime than
previous ones, of greater power, and more val-
iant, since it tears through this veil and carries
off the jewel, which is the soul.

The death of such persons is very gentle and
very sweet, sweeter and more gentle than was
their whole spiritual life on earth. For they die
with the most sublime impulses and delightful
encounters of love. . . .

Egan suggests, beyond this mystical insight's applicability to
the death of every person, that "Theologians should also give
more attention to John's teaching on the ecstatic death of the
purified mystic for a richer theology of the death of Christ."[26]

Practical (Psychosocial) Theology

In what way might our *argumentum ex sanctis* link up
with the struggle for justice and peace, and thus the key
concerns of today's practical theologies? Because the (writing)
saints maintained a profound rootedness in practical life, often deriving their spiritual theology from a process of dis-
cerning the movements in their practical experience, it is
not surprising that some contemporary practical theologians
have turned to them as paradigms of a praxis-oriented style
of theology. The kinds of concerns typical of today's praxis
theologies might likely find in these mystics prototypes of
the style of theology needed for today's practical problems.

South American liberation theology, for example, has
already shown a remarkable rehabilitation of the appeal to
the saints in theology. I first noticed this in Jon Sobrino's

suggestive little study "The Christ of the Ignatian Exercises," appended to his larger *Christology at the Crossroads*. Sobrino is a Jesuit, so it is not surprising that he senses a certain affinity with Loyola. But what is particularly noteworthy is his attempt to learn practical, theological lessons from Ignatius. "Given the praxis-oriented nature of the Exercises, we can readily see that Loyola's conception of the whole Christ will appear more clearly in the kind of praxis he demands in any explicit statements," says Sobrino. Ignatius, then, does not seem to focus on the conciliar or scholastic christologies, but shows a particular sensitivity to "the actual life of Jesus when he sought to effect a change in people's lives." Thus, the special stress on discipleship, the attention to the negative dimension of existence (sin, injustice, and death), discernment as the ability to flesh "out one's inner intentions in history even as Jesus of Nazareth did," the element of conflict in real discipleship as expressed in the Ignatian *agere contra* and the struggle between the two standards, etc. Loyola, if you will, serves as a bridge to the revitalization of the praxis dimensions of the biblical christology. "Thus the Christology of the Exercises is a Christology of the historical Jesus that triggers a concrete form of discipleship structured after the activity of Jesus himself."[27]

I would consider Sobrino typical of the way the consultation of the saints functions in liberation theology. Thus, Leonardo Boff has produced a book-length study of St. Francis of Assisi, bringing a practical sensitivity to Francis similar to Sobrino's. He particularly uncovers Francis' rich theology of fraternity, which is particularly suspicious of hierarchical tendencies toward elitism and oppressiveness. Francis helps Boff refind the "fraternal" implications of Christianity and society. Segundo Galilea consults the Spanish mystics (Ignatius Loyola, Teresa of Avila, and John of the Cross), reading them with a similar liberationist sensitivity. Like Boff,

Galilea is aware that these mystics had "little awareness of the structural problems of society or analysis of their causes." Yet, they are crucial in safeguarding the truly spiritual nature of liberation, for they highlight "the indissoluble relation between interior liberation and social liberation; the need for a mysticism of faith and love in liberation; the value of poverty and austerity in the building of a more just and fraternal society; the awareness of a God who is both liberated and capable of liberating." Especially impressive in Galilea is his rehabilitation of what he calls the "critical consciousness" of the mystics. That is, in them we possess our own Christian exploration of the passions, the irrational, and the night side of human existence, a kind of proto-phenomenology of evil. And this phenomenology extends even to the social surd of human existence: "For them the *world* (as used in the fourth gospel) is the sin of their time and the ambiguity of reality as a source of human servitude."[28]

Consulting the martyrs for theological purposes is also an important trend in practical theology. Gustavo Gutierrez explosively says of the South American martyrs that "their very corpses are subversive." On the one hand, "these martyrs are testifying that there is poverty in Latin America and that the poor are calling the status quo to account." On the other hand, these martyrs raise for us the politically explosive martyrdom of Jesus himself as it is reflected in the "scourged Christs of the Indies."[29] In other words, the sociopolitical sting of christology comes front and center here. The Eastern Orthodox are also undergoing a rehabilitation of the consultation of the martyrs. As Michael Bourdeaux helpfully put it: "Though the world at large still ignores the testimony of the Church under communism, the day cannot now be far away when lessons will be learned and great inspiration will flow back from the persecuted Churches to the

privileged ones to revitalize them." For his own part, Bourdeaux sees flowing from the Russian Christian martyrs a renewed theology of the suffering (Calvary) Jesus, a less passive
Church in secular society, and an intensification of all aspects
of Christian experience, such as the theme of *kenosis* (or self-
abasement) and the emergence of new "startsy" or saints in
Russia.[30]

Finally, we should alert ourselves to the impressive
emergence of a feminist consultation of the saints. This schol-
arship consults the saints in an effort, as Joann Wolski Conn
puts it,

> . . . to recover the general history of women's re-
> ligious experience. Urgent also is the need to tell
> the story of women's leadership. Because mean-
> ing requires imagination, women need to picture
> their own past and have role models to support
> their vision for the future.

In pursuit of this goal, Conn herself has produced a number
of stunning studies of St. Thérèse of Lisieux which balance
and "correct" an all too common view of Thérèse "as the
Pollyanna-type 'good little Sister' who picked up pins for the
love of God and let filthy laundry water splash in her face."
Quite to the contrary, we seem to find in her, given the
context of nineteenth century French Catholicism, a liberationist view of spirituality, a love-theology of the Church at
a time when ecclesiology was quite juridical, and a theology
of heaven and God as radical Love. "Thérèse is a strong,
creative, mature young woman who thought independently
and originally, who could thus give a genuine self in a free
loving relationship to God," says Conn.[31]

Again, Conn's work seems to be representative of the
feminist appropriation of the saints. Conn concentrates upon

Thérèse as a role model for women, and thus particularly challenges the androcentric anthropology of the tradition. Her choice of Thérèse is terribly significant, for the "Little Flower" is an influential model over many women in the Church. Conn's corrective or her "revisionist" view could have explosive implications. Sonya Quitslund's feminist "consultation" of St. Teresa of Avila represents an effort similar to Conn's. Her study represents a truly original effort at interpretation, bringing out the rather explosive "feminist" statements which we actually can find in Teresa. How many of us have read Teresa's *The Way of Perfection* and yet missed the punch in these lines:

> Jesus found more faith and no less love in women
> than in men. . . . Since the world's judges are
> sons of Adam and all of them men, there is no
> virtue in woman that they do not hold suspect. I
> see that these are times in which it would be
> wrong to undervalue virtuous and strong souls,
> even though they are women.

Quitslund has tried to surface Teresa's own feminist sensitivity, showing, like Conn's study, how one's womanness is a positive force in the human-spiritual quest. Quitslund offers a persuasive and subtle interpretation of Teresa's original womb imagery which I have found nowhere else. The more traditional womb imagery is that of the soul nesting in God, and one does find this imagery employed by Teresa (viz., the cocoon image). But in the *Interior Castle* she has God dwelling/nesting in the soul. Here the soul becomes the womb. The first image is a more passive view of the soul; the second, more active, stressing the importance of human responsibility in the spiritual quest. Is Teresa challenging the passive, feminine stereotype common in the tradition?[32]

I think it is important to recognize that these women

are consulting these saints for properly theological reasons. For the experience and theology of these saints challenges the theological tradition's common view of women as passive and subordinate to man. This is a challenge to theological anthropology, ecclesiology, and perhaps even the theology of God. For once women's experience is positively valued, equally with the males', then it becomes possible to draw possible insights into God from the full human experience, men's as well as women's. The feminist consultation of Dame Julian of Norwich's feminist theology is an indication of this important tendency.[33]

As we catch our breath at the end of our tour of contemporary theology, we should be asking ourselves why it is that the saints seem to peek out at us in almost every area of inquiry. In the next chapter we'll wrestle with this question a bit.

Notes

[1]Yves M.-J. Congar, *La Tradition et les traditions: Essai Théologiques* (Paris: Arthème Fayard, 1963), p. 206 (my transl.). Cf. Adalbert Hamman, "Signification doctrinale des Actes des martyrs," *Nouvelle Révue Théologiques* 75 (1953), 739–745, and Réné Latourelle, "La Sainteté Signe de la Révélation," *Gregorianum* XLVI (1965), 36–65. Cf., for example, William Johnston, *The Inner Eye of Love: Mysticism and Religion* (New York: Harper and Row, 1978), for an example of a theologian who wants to relink spirituality and theology.

[2]Karl Rahner, *The Dynamic Element in the Church* (New York: Herder and Herder, 1964), pp. 84–170 at 86.

[3]Hans Urs von Balthasar, *Thérèse of Lisieux*, pp. xxvi, xiii, xv, and "Theology and Sanctity," in his *Word and Redemption: Essays in Theology*, 2 (New York: Herder and Herder, 1965), p. 69. Mon-

ika K. Hellwig, *Understanding Catholicism* (New York: Paulist, 1981), p. 27: "The Church has also established a process of canonization of saints. This pinpoints the recollection of certain lives and the telling of their stories as a means of understanding the implications of the faith." She also views as theological sources, *ibid.*, officially approved religious congregations and movements, and varied spiritual writings, schools, and traditions.

⁴Cf. Bernard Häring, *The Law of Christ: Moral Theology for Priests and Laity*, 2, *Special Moral Theology: Life in Fellowship with God and Fellow Man* (Westminister, MD: Newman, 1963), pp. 417–423 esp., and *Free and Faithful in Christ: Moral Theology for Priests and Laity*, 2, *The Truth Will Set You Free* (New York: Crossroad, 1979), pp. 218–219, 259, 453–456, 439–446 esp. Throughout the three volumes of each of these series Häring consults the saints. James P. Hanigan, *As I Have Loved You: The Challenge of Christian Ethics* (New York: Paulist, 1986), pp. 25–26, sees the heroes and heroines of the faith as moral sources. Philip S. Keane, *Christian Ethics and Imagination: A Theological Inquiry* (New York: Paulist, 1984), esp. pp. 39–44, also integrates the saints and mystics into moral theology. See Walter Conn, *Christian Conversion: A Developmental Interpretation of Autonomy and Surrender* (New York: Paulist, 1986), pp. 158–286, for a fine use of Thomas Merton in moral theology.

⁵Kallistos Ware, "Scholasticism and Orthodoxy: Theological Method as a Factor in the Schism," *Eastern Churches Review* 5 (1973), 16–27 at 20 (citing from Nicholas Zernov) and 21; cf. his "Tradition and Personal Experience in Later Byzantine Theology," *ibid.* 3 (1970), 131–141. Two especially fine works: Vladimir Lossky, *The Mystical Theology of the Eastern Church* (London: James Clarke & Co., 1957), esp. "Introduction: Theology and Mysticism in the Tradition of the Eastern Church," pp. 7–22, and John Meyendorff, *Byzantine Theology: Historical Trends and Doctrinal Themes* (New York: Fordham University, 1974), esp. pp. 7–14. Orthodoxy, of course, tends not to separate moral and systematic and fundamental theology. For a challenging moral theology, largely based on an Orthodox consultation of the mystics, see

Christos Yannaras, *The Freedom of Morality* (Crestwood, New York: St. Vladimir's Seminary, 1984).

[6]Robert C. Neville, *Soldier Sage Saint* (New York: Fordham University, 1978); Geoffrey Wainwright, *Doxology: The Praise of God in Worship, Doctrine and Life: A Systematic Theology* (New York: Oxford, 1980), esp. pp. 109–112, and his "In Praise of God," *Worship* 53 (1979), 496–511 (a summary of his book); Patrick Sherry, *Spirit, Saints, and Immortality* (Albany: SUNY Press, 1984); and Michael Perham, *The Communion of Saints* (London: Alcuin Club/SPCK, 1980), p. 48.

[7]Cf. James M. Gustafson, *Ethics from a Theocentric Perspective*, 1, *Theology and Ethics* (Chicago: University of Chicago, 1981), pp. 136–150, 197–204, 318–320, 327–342, and his "Spiritual Life and Moral Life," in *Theology and Christian Ethics* (Philadelphia: Pilgrim, 1974), pp. 161–176.

[8]I am speaking of the "stress" or "accent" in their thought; obviously this is a personal judgment on my part.

[9]Friedrich von Hügel, *The German Soul* (New York: E. P. Dutton, 1916), p. 209; cf. his great study, *The Mystical Element of Religion as Studied in Saint Catherine of Genoa and Her Friends*, 2 vols. (London: J. M. Dent and Sons, 1961).

[10]A particularly clear statement from Rahner is his "Experience of Transcendence from the Standpoint of Catholic Dogmatics," *Theological Investigations* XVIII (New York: Crossroad, 1983), pp. 173–188 at 176: " . . . mysticism in an explicit experience has . . . a paradigmatic character, an exemplary function, to make clear to the Christian what really happens and is meant when his faith tells him that God's self-communication is given to him in grace and accepted freedom whenever he believes, hopes, and loves." See Harvey Egan, " 'The Devout Christian of the Future Will . . . Be a "Mystic." ' Mysticism and Karl Rahner's Theology," in William J. Kelly, ed., *Theology and Discovery: Essays in Honor of Karl Rahner, S. J.* (Milwaukee, Wisc.: Marquette University, 1980), pp. 139–158; Avery Dulles, *Models of Revelation* (Garden City, N. Y.: Doubleday, 1983), pp. 34, 74–75, 79, 148–150; David Tracy, who regularly refers to mysticism in his *Blessed Rage for*

Order: The New Pluralism in Theology (New York: Seabury, 1975) and *The Analogical Imagination: Christian Theology and the Culture of Pluralism* (New York: Crossroad, 1981): note "Mysticism" in the indexes, p. 268 and p. 466 respectively; Louis Dupré, *The Deeper Life: An Introduction to Christian Mysticism* (New York: Crossroad, 1981); Lossky, *op. cit.*; Kallistos Ware, *The Orthodox Way* (London: Mowbrays, 1979), esp. pp. 12–87; Eric Voegelin, *Anamnesis* (Notre Dame: University of Notre Dame, 1978), pp. 192–199; Paul Tillich, *Systematic Theology*, 1 (Chicago: University of Chicago, 1951), pp. 9, 16, 44, 140–141, 172, 213, 234; Peter Berger, *The Heretical Imperative: Contemporary Possibilities of Religious Affirmation* (Garden City, N.Y.: Doubleday Anchor, 1979): note "Mysticism and mystics" in the index, p. 201. For trinitarian theologies derived (at least partially) from the mystics, see: Von Hügel, *The Mystical Element*, 1, pp. 66–70; John Macquarrie, *In Search of Deity: An Essay in Dialectical Theism* (New York: Crossroad, 1985), pp. 174–175, 193–198; and Meyendorff, pp. 180–190. James P. Mackey, *The Christian Experience of God as Trinity* (London: SCM, 1983), pp. 173–180, challengingly builds upon John of Ruysbroek to argue that trinitarian schemata are only one way to express the divine reality, a way which is valid but limited.

[11]Cf. Egan, *ibid.*; also, Karl Rahner, *On Prayer* (New York: Paulist, 1958), pp. 20–21 (the reference to Bérulle), "Teresa of Avila Doctor of the Church," in his *Opportunities for Faith* (New York: Seabury, 1974), pp. 123–126, and "One Mediator and Many Mediations," *Theological Investigations*, IX (New York: Seabury, 1972), pp. 169–184.

[12]Hans Urs von Balthasar, *The Glory of the Lord: A Theological Aesthetics*, I, *Seeing the Form* (San Francisco: Ignatius/New York: Crossroad, 1982), p. 659. For a helpful introduction, see Medard Kehl and Werner Löser, eds., *The Von Balthasar Reader*, "Saints in the Church" (New York: Crossroad, 1982), pp. 376–407.

[13]Meyendorff, *op. cit.*, pp. 138–139.

[14]Karl Rahner, *Theological Investigations*, IV (Baltimore: Helicon, 1966), p. 110.

[15]Von Balthasar, "Theology and Sanctity," pp. 73–74.

[16]Wolfhart Pannenberg, *Jesus—God and Man* (Philadelphia: Westminister, 1968), p. 340; also Walter Kasper, *Jesus the Christ* (New York: Paulist, 1976), p. 242.

[17]Cf. Meyendorff, *op. cit.*, pp. 151–167, and his *Christ in Eastern Christian Thought* (Washington: Corpus, 1969), esp. pp. 163–166.

[18]William M. Thompson, *The Jesus Debate: A Survey and Synthesis* (New York: Paulist, 1985), pp. 25–26, 32, 61, 192–193, 235, 261, 264–265, 310–320, 323–333, 340. Also see, for creative uses of the mystics in christology, Gerard S. Sloyan, *The Jesus Tradition: Images of Jesus in the West* (Mystic, Connecticut: Twenty-Third Publications, 1986), and George H. Tavard, "The Christology of the Mystics," *Theological Studies* 42 (1981), 561–579.

[19]Cf. Dumitru Staniloae, *Theology and the Church* (Crestwood, N.Y.: St. Vladimir's Seminary Press, 1980), esp. "The Holy Spirit and the Sobornicity of the Church," pp. 45–71; Perham, *op. cit.*, p. 48; Peter Chirico, *Infallibility: The Crossroads of Doctrine* (Kansas City: Sheed Andrews and McMeel/Wilmington, Delaware: Michael Glazier, 1977), pp. 88, 126, 171, 321.

[20]Egan, *op. cit.*, pp. 152, 170–171; cf. pp. 150–152, 170–173, 73–79, and 106–109. There are, of course, many levels of thought in Dante's great *Divine Comedy;* for an interpretation sensitive to the approach I am suggesting, see James Collins, *Pilgrim in Love: An Introduction to Dante and His Spirituality* (Chicago: Loyola University, 1984).

[21]Cf. Karl Rahner, *Foundations of Christian Faith: An Introduction to the Idea of Christianity* (New York: Crossroad, 1978), pp. 434, 435.

[22]St. Teresa of Avila, *The Book of Her Life* 20, 16 *The Collected Works of St. Teresa of Avila*, 1, Kieran Kavanaugh and Otilio Rodriguez, eds. (Washington, D.C.: Institute of Carmelite Studies, 1976), p. 134; cf. also St. John of the Cross, *The Dark Night* 2,6,6; 2,12,1–7.

[23]*The Von Balthasar Reader*, pp. 403–405 at 403–404; cf. his *First Glance at Adrienne von Speyr* (San Francisco: Ignatius,

1981), and "The Descent into Hell," *Chicago Studies* 23 (1984), 223–236. I would consider Von Speyr's "experiences of hell" to be anticipatory implications deduced from her present mystical experiences, in accord with Rahner's eschatological hermeneutics, as mentioned earlier. Cf. Herbert Vorgrimler's critical comment on Von Balthasar's view of universal reconciliation: Vorgrimler sees it as a compensation for the elitism of Von Balthasar's view of the Christian life, echoing Karl Rahner's criticisms of Von Balthasar, in *Understanding Karl Rahner: An Introduction to His Life and Thought* (New York: Crossroad, 1986), pp. 124–125.

[24]John Hick, *Death and Eternal Life* (New York: Harper and Row, 1976), p. 446.

[25]Lossky, pp. 236–249 at 224 and 247.

[26]Egan, *op. cit.*, pp. 201 and 211; the citation from St. John of the Cross: *The Living Flame of Love* 30 *The Collected Works of St. John of the Cross*, Kieran Kavanaugh and Otilio Rodriguez, eds. (Washington, D.C.: Institute of Carmelite Studies, 1973), pp. 591–592.

[27]Jon Sobrino, *Christology at the Crossroads: A Latin American Approach* (Maryknoll, N.Y.: Orbis, 1978), pp. 396–424, at 399, 400, 403, 423.

[28]Cf. Leonardo Boff, "The Need for Political Saints," *Cross Currents* XXX (1980-81), 369–376, and *Saint Francis: A Model for Liberation* (New York: Crossroad, 1982); Segundo Galilea, *The Future of Our Past: The Spanish Mystics Speak to Contemporary Spirituality* (Notre Dame, Indiana: Ave Maria, 1985), pp. 80–81, 49. See Thompson, pp. 24–38, esp. p. 26.

[29]Gustavo Gutierrez, *The Power of the Poor in History: Selected Writings* (Maryknoll, N.Y.: Orbis, 1983), p. 89; cf. pp. 153 and 194–199. Matthew Lamb's *Solidarity with Victims: Toward a Theology of Social Transformation* (New York: Crossroad, 1982) can be read not only as a work taking up an important theme in political theology (viz., the hermeneutics of suspicion forced upon us by history's victims), but also as a sociopolitical consultation of the martyrs. All of this does not so much replace Karl Rahner's view of the martyr's death as the great witness to Christ's ability

to transform death, but surfaces its sociopolitical side. Cf. Rahner "On Martyrdom," in his *On the Theology of Death* (New York: Herder and Herder, 1961), pp. 81–119.

[30]Michael Bourdeaux, *Risen Indeed: Lessons in Faith from the USSR* (Crestwood, N.Y.: St. Vladimir's Seminary Press, 1983), pp. 13, 42, 48, 51, 53, 76; cf. "L'Etat et la religion en U.S.S.R.," *Istina* 26 (1981), Nos. 1–4, and Dimitry Pospielovsky, *The Russian Church under the Soviet Regime 1917–1982* (Crestwood, N.Y.: St. Vladimir's Seminary Press, 1984).

[31]Joann Wolski Conn, "Women's Spirituality: Restriction and Reconstruction," *Cross Currents* 30 (1980), 293–308 and 322 at 302, and "Thérèse of Lisieux from a Feminist Perspective," *Spiritual Life* 28 (1982), 233–239 at 233 and 239; now reprinted in her edited *Women's Spirituality: Resources for Christian Development* (New York: Paulist, 1986), pp. 317–325; Von Balthasar speaks of her "existential theology" in his *Thérèse of Lisieux*, pp. 13–36.

[32]Sonya A. Quitslund, "Elements of a Feminist Spirituality in St. Teresa," in John Sullivan, ed., *Carmelite Studies: Centenary of St. Teresa*, Catholic University Symposium, October 15–17, 1982 (Washington, D.C.: Institute of Carmelite Studies, 1984), pp. 19–50 at 29, citing *The Way of Perfection* 3, 7. Jesús Castellano has written of a *"grito feminista"* (feminist scream) present in St. Teresa, referring esp. to *The Way of Perfection* 4, 1, El Escorial version, in his "Espiritualidad Teresiana: Rasgos y Vivencias," in Alberto Barrientos, ed., *Introducción a La Lectura de Santa Teresa: Obra en colaboración* (Madrid: Editorial de Espiritualidad, 1978), pp. 105–201 at 199.

[33]Cf., for example, Rosemary Radford Ruether, *Sexism and God-Talk: Toward a Feminist Theology* (Boston: Beacon, 1983), pp. 128–129. Cf. also Caroline Walker Bynum, *Jesus as Mother: Studies in the Spirituality of the High Middle Ages* (Berkeley: University of California, 1982).

II

Thinking About Theology's New
Interest in the Saints

I think the last chapter made a fairly convincing case for the view that something like a rehabilitation of the consultation of the saints is underway in today's theology. The "fire" of the mystic seems to be penetrating the "light" of the theologian, if you will. Why is this renaissance happening? Is it symptomatic of important "modulations" in the theological enterprise itself? In this brief chapter I would like to begin an exploration of these questions. However, in a way this entire book will be an attempt to answer these questions.

As I indicated earlier, western theology had tended to ignore the saints and mystics, as well as the martyrs, a trend apparently establishing itself in approximately the fourteenth century. So far as I can tell, scholars generally date the separation of spirituality from theology to this period, at least in the west. Consulting the saints remains somewhat characteristic of Eastern Orthodox theology, although it also knows its period of separation from mystical experience. Still, I would suggest that there is a new stress upon the use of the saints even in eastern theology, a kind of deliberate emphasis upon the hagiographical criteriology as truly distinctive of the Orthodox in contrast to western theological methods. With respect to the Reformation heritage, at the very least we can say that the appeal to the saints, mystics, and martyrs is certainly somewhat novel: this appeal tends to be rather more sedate and mute until relatively recently.[1]

My suggestion would be that we look to larger trends within theology and culture as the probable explanation for this rehabilitation of the saints. After all, the writings (often autobiographies) of the saints and mystics offer a potentially rich source for an *experiential* approach to religious and Christian realities. An age like our own, which since the Enlightenment has stressed experience as the norm and source of all human knowledge, might just find in the saints and mystics a bridge to a renewed experiential grounding of religion. For the saints don't just mime a theology: they live it and explore it experientially. To use von Balthasar's phrase, they present us with a "supernatural phenomenology."[2] This is why, I think, the mystics have often been a favored source for the study of religious claims in modern times (think of William James' *The Varieties of Religious Experience*).

Eric Voegelin, for example, has pointed to Jean Bodin's exploration of mysticism already in the sixteenth century as an experiential alternative to the loss of transcendence. He mentions Bergson's appreciation of the mystics as a more recent example.[3] Von Hügel could serve as another example of a thinker who saw the mystics as "amongst the great benefactors of our race." Why? Because "Religion, at least among the mystics (and I believe that, on this point at least, the mystics merely dive deeper into and bring out more explicitly the sap or the central core of the religious passion), consists centrally in the sense of Presence—the sense of an overflowing Existence distinct from our own and in the adoration of the same." Von Hügel felt that the age in which he lived, experiential though it was, ran the danger of an excessively restrictive view of experience which a consultation of the mystics might correct: "We live in times . . . of such excess of analysis over synthesis—that it is in the air all around us to ask questions, to poke about . . . where to become and to be, to produce reality, to adore and to will, and to see things in the large and upon the whole, and at their best, is what we all require."[4] In tune with the primal promptings of our age, the mystics are deeply experiential. At the same time, they exemplify a vision of human experience that is wider than simply sense experience. In this sense, they might serve as a bridge for people today, a "benefactor," to use Von Hügel's colorful word. If we keep all of this in mind, we can see that the "turn to the saints" is of a piece with other "experiential" approaches in modern theology: the "revisionist" model of Tracy, transcendental Thomism's search for the conditions of the possibility within human experience of religious beliefs, story theologies, the use of phenomenological methods within theology, etc. As we proceed, we might fruitfully ask ourselves what the special strengths of a turning to the mystics might be vis-à-vis other experiential theological methods.

The irruption of the mystics, and especially the martyrs, in practical theologies (sociopolitical and feminist) needs to be related to the larger cultural and theological factors grounding the emergence of those theological fields. If we cast a glance back to the authors we all too quickly surveyed, clearly the authority of the saints seems to be invoked for varied motives. Attention to praxis, to experience in the mode of reflectively thought out action rather than simply theory, is surely an important factor. The practical theologians turn to the martyrs and mystics as allies in the quest for a theology which will let itself learn lessons from praxis. Perhaps these practical theologians sense a kind of affinity with the martyrs and mystics: both at times have had to struggle against the theological theories "in possession" by attending to the praxis of their experience.[5]

Attunement to praxis then brings with it surprising revelations, which perhaps account for the varied ways in which the saints find themselves "consulted." Feminists find more liberating models in some of the mystics than in some of the models held out by the "powers in possession" or the reigning theological anthropologies. Perhaps, too, they find paradigms of their felt need to critique the night side of the tradition. Liberation theologians find in the martyrs spiritual allies in their own struggle to expose corrupt regimes and practices. The martyrs theologically legitimate this: some forms of subversion are making a theological statement. All practical theologians find in the great writing mystics profound probings of human evil, of the irrationalities of human existence, of the passions, etc. A kind of "supernatural pathology" surfaces, in other words, which aids the practical theologian in his or her own "hermeneutics of suspicion" vis-à-vis the tradition and contemporary secular and religious ideologies. In some respects, the mystical phenomenology of pathology is superior to other attempted analyses (either in the political liberal or socialist traditions), for it possesses an unparalleled exploration of the deceptions of human motivation and idolatry. We have seen that the mystics were aware of the social surd/evil of human existence, in their use of the "Johannine" notion of the "world." In all of these respects, the turn to the martyrs and mystics aids the practical theologian in developing a quite uniquely Christian appropriation of the lessons of the so called "late" or "second" Enlightenment, which critiqued the optimism of the first one.[6]

Attunement to the harsh summons of a liberating praxis also has its dangers, its own shadow side, at least for the Christian. As one engages in the conflict with injustice, one often meets with rejection, bitter disappointments (sometimes from the hands of the churches), and even a growing rage within oneself. One can feel estranged, even from a supporting Divine Mystery. Gregory Baum has called this "a loss of religious substance" on the part of many "engaged Christians." To avoid this, he powerfully suggests:

> The Christian church that at this time is trying to understand its mission in terms of solidarity and liberation must engage in contemplation of the mystery of God as matrix and enabler in human life and as forward movement in history. In the Christian perspective, action equals passion. While we see, we are being enlightened, while we act, we are being carried forward, while we love, we are being saved from selfishness, and while we embrace all people in solidarity, we are being freed inwardly to cross one boundary after another.[7]

Might I suggest that a mystical attunement to the Divine Mystery helps one avoid the disastrous pitfalls of both pessimism and utopianism? Pessimism, because no matter how horrible the resistance one encounters, one knows a more powerful, transcendent source of strength. Utopianism, because openness to the Mystery frees one from idolatrous ideologies, fanaticisms, and gnostic arrogance. Perhaps today's practical theologians sense something of all of this in the martyrs, saints, and mystics increasingly consulted by them.[8] Is this an aspect of the attractiveness of the mystics?

A final factor which might have contributed to the increasing prominence of at least the mystics in the consciousness of today's theologians is the growing encounter with the venerable religions of the Far East: Hinduism, Buddhism, etc. As we peoples of the earth grow more sensitized to one another, through communications media, and other forms of political, cultural, and economic interdependence, we allow the religious traditions of the non-Christian religions to question and even enrich us. In part, this has brought a heightened awareness of the rich explorations into mysticism typical of these religions. For these religions, "theology" is always rooted in practical, spiritual experience. Oftentimes, one learns through a complex process of discipleship, involving frequent "consultation" of the "masters," of both past and present. As Christian theologians find themselves drawn into the transcultural dialogue, they find that their understanding of what it means "to consult the saints" undergoes a corresponding cross-culturalization. Raimundo Panikkar and John Dunne, Thomas Merton and Mircea Eliade— surely these are some of the better known pioneers and prototypes of a development only now irrupting in western theology.[9]

Notes

[1]See Perham and Maloney.

[2]Von Balthasar, *Thérèse of Lisieux*, p. xviii.

[3]Voegelin, p. 195.

[4]Von Hügel, *The Mystical Element of Religion*, 2, p. 340; *The Reality of God and Religion and Agnosticism* (London: J. M. Dent & Sons, 1931), p. 71; and *Letters to a Niece* (New York: E. P. Dutton, 1950), p. 134. Cf. the very fine study of Joseph P. Whelan, *The Spirituality of Friedrich von Hügel* (New York: Newman/Paulist, 1971).

[5]Cf. Walter Kasper, ed., *Sie suchten die Wahrheit: Heilige Theologen* (Mainz: Matthias-Grünewald, 1985), his "Theologie und Heiligkeit," pp. 7–16, esp. 12–16, for some helpful comments on praxis in the saints who were theologians.

[6]Cf. H. Stuart Hughes, *Consciousness and Society: The Reorientation of European Social Thought 1890–1930* (New York: Vintage, 1958), for a fuller study of the late Enlightenment.

[7]Gregory Baum, *Religion and Alienation: A Theological Reading of Sociology* (New York: Paulist, 1975), p. 291. It seems to me

that Johann Baptist Metz, *Faith in History and Society: Toward a Practical Fundamental Theology* (New York: Crossroad, 1980), and Gustavo Gutierrez, *We Drink from Our Own Wells: The Spiritual Journey of a People* (Maryknoll, N.Y.: Orbis, 1984), show a special sensitivity to this. Analogously, Eric Voegelin seems most sensitive to this in the field of political theory in general; cf. esp. his "The Consciousness of the Ground," *op. cit.*, pp. 147–174.

[8]Thompson, pp. 190–191.

[9]Cf., among others: Raimundo Panikkar, *The Intrareligious Dialogue* (New York: Paulist, 1978) and *Myth, Faith and Hermeneutics: Cross-Cultural Studies* (New York: Paulist, 1979); John Dunne, *The Way of All the Earth* (New York: Macmillan, 1972); Thomas Merton, *Mystics and Zen Masters* (New York: Delta, 1967); Mircea Eliade, *The Sacred and the Profane: The Nature of Religion* (New York: Harper Torchbooks, 1951), perhaps the most succinct statement of his views. Also cf. Guilford Dudley III, *Religion on Trial: Mircea Eliade and His Critics* (Philadelphia: Temple University, 1977), and Seymour Cain, "Mircea Eliade: Attitudes Toward History," *Religious Studies Review* 6 (1980), 13–16. An interesting cross-cultural study of the saints is T. M. P. Mahadevan, ed., *A Seminar on Saints: Papers Presented at the Second Seminar of the Union for the Study of the Great Religions (India)* (Madras, India: G. S. Press, 1960). This last reference is thanks to the courtesy of Raimundo Panikkar.

III

Soundings in the Tradition

What light might the ecclesial and theological tradition cast upon the apparently rich trend of consulting the saints? Because theology, as many of us understand it, is always a developing conversation between the theory and praxis of both the tradition and our contemporary concerns or experience, it is important to probe the tradition for its possible insights. The contemporary consultation of the saints, mystics, and martyrs is not a peculiarly modern phenomenon. It forms a part, sometimes subterranean and sometimes more dominant, of the growing tradition, which now offers this strategy to us as we struggle with our own present concerns.[1]

Two trends would seem to run through the tradition: a relatively constant, but not often reflected upon, consultation of the saints; and an occasional, theological analysis of (or "second level reflection upon") what it means to consult the saints. For example, St. Paul says, "Imitate me as I imitate Christ" (1 Cor 11:1). This Pauline text argues in a way similar to the famous text of Hebrews 11, which looks to the "faith of the ancients" as an example of the meaning of faith itself. Both cases are New Testament examples of the *argumentum ex sanctis*. Both assume the validity of the procedure of consulting the saints, but offer little, if any, second level reflection upon it. An incarnational religion like Christianity, which believes that God mediates the divine presence in a human way, is particularly open to the notion of holy mediators in any case. And the notion was a commonly accepted

41

one in the world's religions. As Geoffrey Wainwright put it, we are dealing with the "Christian instance of the principle expressed in general religious terms by Ninian Smart: 'The holiness possessed by the holy man is derivative. . . . One can as it were worship God by reference to the saints, for they reflect God's holiness.' "[2] Given the widespread acceptance of this notion, it is not surprising that we do not find explicitly theological reflection upon it in the Scriptures. The consultation of the saints, such as we have it in the New Testament, simply continues and perhaps intensifies the Hebraic belief that Yahweh's holiness flows through his people: "Be holy, for I, the Lord your God, am holy" (Lev 19:2). Because the faithful of Israel and of Jesus are holy (Dt 7:6; Ps 50:5; Is 4:3; Mt 27:52; 1 Pt 1:15–16; 2 Cor 13:13; Acts 9:13, etc.), and some are particularly holy (cf. esp. Is. 4:3 and Jude 3), they become sources of revelation. Consulting the saints is a corollary of believing in and "consulting" a God who mediates the divine presence through the faithful generally, through special mediators, and Christians believe, explosively through Jesus.

Generally, until the later medieval period, there was a lived unity between theology and spirituality, or "science" and "sanctity." Occasionally we meet with statements pointing out that the saints (in a special sense the holy ones) should be consulted, but in general theology is thought to flow from the living experience of sanctity. Again, this is probably why there is little second order reflection upon our theme: it forms a part of the *Zeitgeist*. As St. Augustine understood it, for example, theology was the highest form of wisdom, and *Hominis sapientia pietas est*.[3] Von Balthasar holds that it was only the epoch after Albert, Bonaventure, Thomas, and possibly Scotus which "saw the disappearance of the 'complete' theologian . . . the theologian who is also a saint."[4] Harvey Egan has written rather beautifully of the interpenetration between mysticism and theology in the great patristic writers. This was their "secret," for they "wrote from what they had seen with the eyes of their spirit and loved from the depths of their hearts." This kind of theology also "often led others to experience with lively faith and unction Christianity's great mysteries."[5]

A similar *perichoresis* between theology and sanctity characterizes the great scholastics. St. Thomas Aquinas linked the scientific (= theology) and the affective (spiritual experience): "In other sciences, therefore, it suffices that a man be perfect according to his intellect; in this one, however, he is required to be perfect intellectually and affectively. . . ." And with Thomas we even find the beginnings of some second order reflection upon our theme of consulting the saints (or the "just" in Thomas' terminology). In his *Commentary on Romans* he develops an extensive essay on the "special" ways in which God acts in the lives of the just; namely, through a special care, a special cult, and through special effects upon those who encounter the just. And he holds, citing Augustine, "that the understanding of sacred scripture can be understood from the actions of the saints. . . ."[6]

St. Bonaventure, to take the other great "scholastic," also linked theology and spirituality. In his *Itinerarium* he tells us that he wants to follow "the example of the most blessed Father Francis" and that he does not want his reader to think "that it suffices to read without unction, speculate without devotion, investigate without wonder, examine without exultation, work without piety . . . see without wisdom divinely inspired." In an essay on the theology of created grace he argues that the thesis that grace is a reality conforming and assimilating humans to God is the "more secure" of the possible theological views because it agrees with the "community of teachers, both the words of the commentators and the piety of the saints."[7] Here there is an explicit reference to the saints as theological teachers, but no real second order reflection on the theme. Other occasional references to our theme of consulting the saints are found in Augustine, Vincent of Lerins, and Gregory the Great. We will let Augustine's statement serve as the representative citation. In arguing against the Priscillian interpretation of the commandment not to lie he claims that "a correct understanding of the precept may be obtained from the deeds of the just."[8]

We meet with more extensive reflection upon our theme in the thought of St. Gregory Palamas, the fourteenth century Greek Orthodox theologian. His is perhaps the most sustained treatment of our issue in the tradition, so far as I can tell. Gregory Palamas is increasingly becoming known in the West as one of the great explorers in Byzantine theology, offering a richly christocentric theology at once indebted to late Hellenism and yet critical of the latter's dualistic tendencies. This christocentric quality of his work seems to have been the key factor behind his critique of a style of theology which seemed to stress an exaggerated notion of divine transcendence. His defense of the true deification of Byzantine mystics rests upon God's real, incarnational entry into human existence. Theologian-bishop Kallistos Ware sees Palamas' stress upon the experience of the mystics as a corollary of his incarnationalism. And as his incarnationalism is intense, so is his appeal to the saints. "St. Gregory Palamas . . . in his *Triads* regularly invokes the living experience of holy men: it is they who are the real theologians; as for those who are trained to analyse and discuss, who are skilled in the use of words and logic, they are at best theologians in an altogether secondary and derivative sense."[9] In my own reading of the English (edited) version of the *Triads*, I have counted approximately fifty places where Palamas explicitly consults the experience of the saints/mystics.

The *Triads*—Palamas' defense of hesychasm against the philosopher Barlaam—seems to appeal to the experience (*pēra*) of the saints in such a way that that appeal becomes the fundamental theological criterion: "All these things become clear by experience," he tells us. Palamas distinguishes between those who enjoy pēra, the direct personal experience of God's uncreated presence ("energies"); those lacking this personal experience but relying upon those who possess it; and those both lacking it and refusing to rely upon those who do have it. He condemns the last, praises the humility of the second group, but considers only the first as the theologians in the plenary sense. "It is our purpose to communicate the teaching on the light of grace of those long-revered saints whose wisdom comes from experience, proclaiming that 'such is the teaching of Scripture.' "

Interestingly, and I think importantly, Gregory consults not only the saints of the past, but those of his own time. He does refer to the "ancients," but he seems to mean writers as late as the tenth and even the thirteenth centuries (namely, Sts. Symeon the New Theologian and Nikiphoros the Hesychast). But he goes beyond this and appeals to people of his own time whom he knows personally and who have taught him (namely, Metropolitan Theoliptos of Philadelphia, Patriarch Athanasios of Constantinople, and others). Thus, when Palamas asks "Do you not see how strictly our views accord with those of the saints?" he has in mind the experience of saints spanning both past and present.[10]

Something else we notice in Palamas is that he seems to speak interchangeably of consulting the saints and of consulting experience (*pēra*). An "appeal to the saints" is an "appeal to experience." "Experience" as understood expansively in a theocentric perspective, of course. This links up with the previous point: "people of experience" are not limited to the past (do we tend to associate the "saints" with the past?) but found in our contemporary setting. At the same time, the stress upon experience underscores what Palamas regards as the real significance of the saint (either of the past or present): they embody the Divine Presence (= deification).[11]

Interestingly, I have encountered a similar "appeal to experience" in some of the saints/mystics with whom I am most familiar. For example, St. Teresa of Avila says that "There was nothing I understood until His Majesty gave me understanding through experience." This citation is from her *Life*, in which I have counted approximately eighty such references to her own experience. Another, particularly clear citation, this time from her *Spiritual Testimonies:*

> The presence of the three Persons is so impossi-
> ble to doubt that it seems one experiences what
> St. John says, that they will make their abode in
> the soul. God does this not only by grace but
> also by His presence, because he wants to give
> the experience of this presence. It brings with it
> an abundance of indescribable blessings, espe-
> cially the blessing that there is no need to go in
> search of reflections in order to know that God is
> there.[12]

Jean Baruzi, in his classic study of St. John of the Cross, had noted a similar "appeal to experience" in John. For example, to take but a couple of examples, John speaks of "the remarkable presence of the Beloved" which the mystic "experiences," and says "the delight of God's glory is experienced and enjoyed in the substance of the soul now transformed in Him."[13] It is not surprising that these mystics are so "experiential." For them, theology is rooted in the living experience of spirituality. When they speak of experience, they ultimately have in mind the experience of sanctity.

Before closing this brief section on the tradition, let me mention two further ways in which the consultation of the saints could be said to show up in the tradition. One of these ways, of course, is the Church's liturgy, which in its commemoration of the saints implicitly looks to the saints as paradigms of the Christian life. The liturgy even occasionally explicitly recognizes the saints as doctrinal and theological sources, rather than simply more generally as *exempla vitae*. Wainwright's important study on the liturgy is sensitive to this:

> Saints can also be prized for having discerned, taught and transmitted what is held to be the saving faith in its true form. The commemoration of the doctors of the Church brings dogma self-consciously to the very heart of the eucharistic anaphora in the liturgy of the . . . Orthodox Syrian Church of the East: "Again we remember those who have before us fallen asleep in holiness and taken repose in the abode of the saints, and who maintained and delivered and entrusted to us the one apostolic and uncorrupt faith."[14]

This liturgical consultation of the "doctored" saints is a specific manifestation of the axiom *lex orandi lex credendi*. Ultimately this axiom reduces itself to what we are calling the consultation of the saints, for to appeal to the witness of prayer (= *lex orandi*) is finally to appeal to the people who embody that prayer (=the community of saints).[15]

Mention of the *lex orandi* naturally brings to mind the

tradition of the *sensus fidelium*, the unerring truthfulness of the faithful people in the Church. Grounded on the Johannine texts of the Spirit's anointing with truth (cf. Jn 2:20, 27; 1 Jn 2), and rehabilitated by the Second Vatican Council ("The body of the faithful as a whole, anointed as they are by the Holy One . . . cannot err in matters of belief"), this tradition teaches and even urges us to look beyond simply doctrinal propositions to the full range of potential sources of divine revelation: the faithful as a whole includes the clergy and laity, those who are the "doctors"-theologians, and those who are the "saints" in an intensive way, together with the vehicles of expression used by these people: the Scriptures, teachings, autobiographies, magisterial decrees, liturgy, prayer, art, and lived experience in general. Here we have a second way in which the consultation of the saints emerges, for it is of a piece with the *sensus fidelium* itself.[16]

As we can see from this all too brief survey, the consultation of the saints is a rich theme in the tradition. Until the growing rationalism of western theology in the late medieval period, it forms a normal part of theological methodology. It is perhaps even more common in Eastern Orthodox theology, as we have seen, Palamas being one of its greatest expositors. But for the most part the tradition is rather more suggestive than explicit on our theme. Consulting the saints forms a part of the Christian *Zeitgeist*. Only when the experience of the saints is called into question (as in the case of Barlaam's attacks upon Gregory Palamas), or when the scholastic theology seems inadequate, and the mystic must then appeal to her or his own experience (as seems the case with Teresa of Avila and John of the Cross)—only then does it seem that we get a somewhat more detailed analysis of our theme or at least some kind of explicit appeal to experience itself as a norm in theology. Let us turn, then, to some "contemporary soundings."

Notes

[1]One will notice the underlying view of theology as a hermeneutical conversation between the tradition and the concerns of our contemporary experience. On this, cf. my *The Jesus Debate*, pp. 45–89, and the works of Tracy.

[2]Wainwright, p. 109, citing Ninian Smart, *The Concept of Worship*, p. 48.

[3]*Enchiridion* 2 (PL 40:231).

[4]Von Balthasar, "Theology and Sanctity," p. 57. Cf. François Vandenbroucke, "Le Divorce entre Théologie et Mystique: Ses Origines," *Nouvelle Révue Théologique* 72 (1950), 372–389.

[5]Egan, p. 375.

[6]*In V. Heb.* 2, 273, as translated by Kieran Conley, *A Theology of Wisdom: A Study in St. Thomas* (Dubuque, Iowa: Priory, 1963), p. 91; *In Ep. Rom.* 1, 5 (Vivès, 20:302, for the citation, my translation).

[7]Saint Bonaventure, *The Mind's Road to God*, George Boas, transl. (Indianapolis: Bobbs-Merrill, 1953), pp. 4–5; *II Sent.* 26, 1, 2, Concl. (Vivès, 3:244, my translation). Note the comment of M.-D. Chenu: "The *sancti* are the Fathers of the Church (the word *Patres* [Fathers], in XIIIth century vocabulary, refers rather to the members of a council) whose testimony holds sway in religious matters" (*Toward Understanding Saint Thomas* [Chicago: Henry Regnery, 1964], p. 138). Chenu is referring to the medieval usage.

[8]St. Augustine, *Lying* 15, 26–27 (*Saint Augustine: Treatises on Various Subjects, Fathers of the Church* 16 [New York, 1952], pp. 88–89). Cf. Vincent of Lerins, *Commonitorium* 28 (PL 50, 675); Gregory the Great, *Homiliae in Hiezechihelem Prophetam* X, 38 (CCSL 142:163). See Congar, pp. 206 and 316n99 for some of these references; the latter incorrectly refers to Augustine's *Contra Mendacium* when it should be to the *Mendacium* 15, 26–27, as I have noted above. Interestingly, there was some discussion at the Council of Trent of partially explaining the Catholic understanding of justification by appealing to some of the saints; viz., David, Paul, Augustine. It was felt that the practical nature of justification made such an appeal especially appropriate. On the issue of the possi-

bility of knowing with certitude that one is saved, at least by a special revelation, appeal to St. Francis was discussed. On this see Jaroslav Pelikan, *The Christian Tradition*, 4, *Reformation of Church and Dogma (1300–1700)* (Chicago: University of Chicago, 1984), pp. 280 and 289, referring to *Concilium Tridentinum* 12:614–615 and 5:642–643. Appropriately, Pelikan thinks that appeal should also have been made to the experience of Martin Luther for an understanding of justification.

[9]Kallistos Ware, "Scholasticism and Orthodoxy," 20. I have used Gregory Palamas, *The Triads* (New York: Paulist, 1983).

[10]Palamas, II.ii.9 (p. 51); II.iii.15 (p. 59); Kallistos Ware, "Tradition and Personal Experience in Late Byzantine Theology," 140, referring to *Triads* I.ii.12 (found only in J. Meyendorff, ed., *Spicilegium Sacrum Lovaniense* [30–31: Louvain, 1959]), for how Palamas refers to saints of past and present; III.ii.10 (p. 97).

[11]Cf. esp. Kallistos Ware, "Tradition and Personal Experience in Late Byzantine Theology"; A. M. Allchin, "The Appeal to Experience in the Triads of St. Gregory Palamas," in F. L. Cross, ed., *Studia Patristica* 8 (*Texte und Untersuchungen* xciii: Berlin, 1966), pp. 323–328; P. Miquel, "Grégoire Palamas, Docteur de l'Experience," *Irenikon* 37 (1964), 227–237. Important studies on Palamas: John Meyendorff, *A Study of Gregory Palamas* (London: Faith, 1964); Georgios I. Mantzaridis, *The Deification of Man: St. Gregory Palamas and the Orthodox Tradition* (Crestwood, NY: St. Vladimir's Seminary, 1984); and *Eastern Churches Review* IX (1977), No's. 1–2.

[12]St. Teresa of Avila, *The Book of Her Life* 22, 3 (p. 145); *Spiritual Testimonies* 9 (*ibid.*, p. 365). Cf. Jesús Castellano, "Espiritualidad Teresiana," pp. 107–117, for some helpful comments on the experiential character of St. Teresa's theology.

[13]I am referring to Jean Baruzi, *Saint Jean de la Croix et le Problème de l'Experience Mystique* (Paris: Felix Alcan, 1931), esp. pp. 231–297. For the citations from John: *The Spiritual Canticle* 12, 5; 22, 5 (*The Collected Works*, pp. 455 and 498).

[14]Wainwright, p. 496n282, citing *The Service Book of the Holy Qurbana*.

[15]The most extensive treatment I have seen is in *ibid.*, pp. 218–283.

[16]See Newman, *On Consulting the Faithful in Matters of Doctrine*, John Coulson, ed. (New York: Sheed and Ward, 1961). Johannes-Baptist Metz and Edward Schillebeeckx, eds., *The Teaching Authority of the Believers, Concilium* 180 (1985), No. 4; and my "Sensus Fidelium and Infallibility," *American Ecclesiastical Review* 167 (1973), 450–486.

IV

Soundings in Current Theology

M ore often than not contemporary theologians consult the saints rather than reflect upon why they should so consult them. But there are some significant developments in the area of a second level reflection upon our *argumentum ex sanctis*, and in any case there are a number of "hard" questions which it is now time to ask. Let us try to move through the key issues one by one.

1. The Basic Approach

So far as I can tell, current scholars focusing upon our theme in a second order manner tend to dwell upon the "experiential" dimension of the appeal to sanctity. As we have seen, this continues the tradition of St. Gregory Palamas and those western mystics like St. Teresa of Avila and St. John of the Cross who ground their spiritual theology in the lived experience of holiness. This is also congenial to the heightened methodological atmosphere of contemporary theology, which attempts various kinds of experiential mediations of the tradition. Harvey Egan, one of Karl Rahner's best American interpreters and deeply influenced by Rahner's own spiritually-influenced theology, is nicely representative of this basic line of argumentation: ". . . the most significant reason for focusing upon the important Christian mystics and saints as an indispensable source of theology is the depth and clarity of their experience of God and the dramatic way in which they have lived the mysteries of the life, death, and resurrection of Jesus Christ." In this sense, they are the "creative exemplars in the history of holiness."[1] Behind Egan's helpful statement, we can catch the "glow" of Rahner's well-known view that the existence of the saints demonstrates that God's offer of salvation is not only a possibility but a reality within history, effectively transforming human lives and human destiny.[2]

When we say that it is *the experience* of the saints which bestows theological importance upon them, we have in mind a properly theological notion of experience. "Experience" means varied things, but the reality of the saints teaches us that it cannot be limited to sense experience alone. Experience knows many levels, including that of openness to and communion with the Divine Mystery, and these other levels are every bit as real as simple sense experience. It is this "hard" reality of these deeper levels which makes of the saints explorers of the depths of human experience, sometimes against their own choice. To paraphrase Von Balthasar, they are "supernatural phenomenologists." To return to Von Hügel, who still remains somewhat incomparable in this area, the saints and mystics are "amongst the great benefactors of our race" who "merely dive deeper into and bring out more explicitly the sap or the central core of the religious passion. . . ."[3] A notion of experience influenced by the living experience of the saints teaches theologians that we need not shrink human experience needlessly. It is quite fluid and elastic, because it remains open to the Mystery of the Transcendent Itself. Here, I think, is the great source of the "authority" of the saints, the martyrs, and the mystics, particularly if we are predisposed to view the ultimate origin of religion as the human experience of divine revelation. Let me add that this experiential approach to the saints nicely corresponds to the biblical view, expressed earlier, that the consultation of the saints is a corollary of believing in the incarnation, of a God mediating the divine presence in human experience.

Before moving to our next issue, let me mention John Meyendorff's interesting "epistemological" translation of what we have just said. He, too, speaks of Byzantine theology as possessing an "experiential nature." "The true theologian," he says, "was the one who saw and experienced the content of his theology; and this experience was considered to belong not to the intellect alone (although the intellect was not excluded from its perception), but to the 'eyes of the Spirit,' which place the whole man—intellect, emotions, and even senses—in contact with divine existence." It is this experiential cast of Byzantine theology which makes it into a "contemplative *theoria*," as understood especially by the Cappadocian Fathers. The notion of revelation is more than propositional here: not a "rational deduction from 'revealed' premises," but rather "a vision experienced by the saints." Meyendorff has drawn the epistemological consequences from this: "The really important implication of this attitude concerns the very notion of Truth, which is conceived, by the Byzantines, not as a concept which can be expressed adequately in words or developed rationally, but as God Himself—personally present and met in the Church in His very personal identity."[4] Could we say that different models of "experience" imply different models of "truth"? Sense experience alone perhaps generates a "picture" or "representational" model of truth (which Meyendorff seems to speak of here as "conceptual"). A hagiographical model of truth, corresponding to a widened and non-restrictive notion of experience, perhaps generates what contemporary theologians at times call a "disclosure" or a "transformational" model of truth. Reality is disclosed rather than pictured; and it transforms the person inside out. In other words, the vision (=

disclosure) and praxis (= transformation) of the saint births a new notion of truth.

2. Two Possible Corollaries

Karl Rahner had suggested that one of the elements distinguishing the "canonized" saint from the "saints" in the wider biblical sense is that they in some way initiate the new in Christian history: "They are the initiators and the creative models of the holiness which happens to be right for, and is the task of, their particular age."[5] A number of other authors have brought out this element of creative novelty in the saints and mystics. We see this reflected in Egan's notion that they are the "creative exemplars in the history of holiness." Von Balthasar, too, has spoken of the "special, representative" saint who derives importance and even greatness from his or her "new charisma" for the Church. Richard Woods has helpfully spoken of the mystics as the "pioneers" searching for new horizons of human attainment and as the "precursors" actually embodying that attainment. Their purgation or dark night of "surfacing, clarifying and appraising those values, ideas, beliefs and patterns of behavior" which will be most helpful to humanity's forward movement is the form of their new charism.[6] If all of this be true, then we are presented with a further reason for the importance of the saints as precisely theological sources. For theology's task is always one of mediating *to the present* the Christian tradition, striving to support the Church's task of incarnating the gospel in every age.

My own suggestion at this point is that this "approach from novelty" ultimately seems to be a variant of the basic experiential approach explained earlier. The saint or mystic can disclose new human and Christian possibilities because of the depth with which the mystic embodies and explores the possibilities of human experience. Living experience at a hagiographical depth means remaining open to as full a range of human-Christian experience as possible, refusing to needlessly restrict experience's range. Relevant to this discussion is an enormously rich hermeneutical discussion of the notion of "experience" in Hans-Georg Gadamer's *Truth and Method*. To repeat the whole matter here would be to ask too much of both reader and publisher. But perhaps the heart of the matter is found in the following two sentences: "The truth of experience always contains an orientation towards new experience. That is why a person who is called 'experienced' has become such not only through experiences, but is also open to new experiences." Gadamer wants to say that the person of experience is "radically undogmatic" or non-gnostic. His or her former experiences and openness to those experiences equips him or her to learn anew. Only this kind of non-dogmatic person can really enjoy genuinely new experiences. This kind of depth of lived experience seems to characterize the great saints and mystics, I would suggest.[7]

Some writers draw a further, even more radical conclusion from their study of the saints. It is what I would call the "maximalist variant" of the appeal to experience as the basic ground for the consultation of the saints in theology. Egan says, for example, that the Christian mystics and saints "are the truly Christian geniuses whose lives manifest the full blossoming of Christian existence." We have also seen how some Eastern Orthodox theologians consider the saints to be the final criterion in theology. But von Balthasar is perhaps the most bold. He calls the theologian-saints, at least, "complete personalities" who are "beyond questioning." They "reproduced the fullness of the Church's teaching, and their teaching the fullness of the Church's life."[8]

This seems to be the kind of intuition that lies behind the notion that the saint or mystic is an eschatological sign:

an indication of the full blossoming of existence that awaits us in the communion of saints. The Second Vatican Council has spoken eloquently on this theme: "For when we look at the lives of those who have faithfully followed Christ, we are inspired with a new reason for seeking the city which is to come (Heb 13:14; 11:10). . . . [God] "speaks to us in them, and gives us a sign of His kingdom, to which we are powerfully drawn, surrounded as we are by so many witnesses (cf. Heb 12:1). . . ."[9] I want now to suggest that the connection between "maximalist" views of the saints and eschatology is important, because the "logic" lying behind both seems to be the same. For example, it is widely believed among theologians that eschatological beliefs are not exact forecasts of our ultimate destiny, but futuristic and somewhat imaginative extrapolations from the past and present experiences of Christians, especially the Jesus event. Eschatological "knowledge" flows from our experience, in other words, searching that experience for significant clues about our final destiny. It is a true, but humble, inexact, analogous, and imaginative kind of knowledge. So, too, to speak of the saints as the "complete persons" or the "full blossoming of human life" is to make statements flowing from our experience of their depth and intensity. The level of the experience lived by the saints seems to us so profound that we trust that it provides us with some kind of indication of that eschatological fullness for which we long. Such statements are extrapolations from the lives of the saints and stand under an "eschatological proviso": they are humble, inexact, and only analogous indications of the final future whose exact shape we can only imagine.

3. The Praxis Dimension

I indicated earlier that the term "experience" is an enormously elastic one, embracing many levels. The renewed emphasis upon "praxis," chiefly through the stimulation of political and liberation theologies, reminds us of one of these levels. Let us call "praxis" experience in the mode of action that is purposive, reflected upon. I believe that is the sense that "praxis" generally carries in current theology. Here praxis is a dimension of experience (some authors don't differentiate the two), highlighting the action component rather than the meaning component of experience. Action seems to be as basic as meaning in our experience: we do and we speculate simultaneously, and each feeds upon the other, enriching and critiquing each other. Practical theologians often say that practice does not simply follow theory, as its mere application, but is a coequal partner with theory in human experience. One of the classical dangers of a theology cut off from spirituality is precisely that it becomes too airy and theoretical, unanchored in praxis. Such theory can derail into ideology, unless it allows itself to be stretched and enriched by practical experience. Of course, it works the other way too: praxis needs the constant enrichment of theory lest it derail into fanaticism. But for now our focus is on praxis.

I believe we have shown above that one of the major contributions of consulting the saints, martyrs, and mystics is their mooring in praxis. Often they remain in touch with praxis and develop their theology by attending to the lessons of praxis. And at times they seem to do this as a conscious alternative to the "ideological" theology reigning at the time. This praxis-side of the saints can mean various things, of course, and I think we are only beginning to explore the rich possibilities here. In the most general sense, the saints and mystics provide us with a specifically Christian notion of praxis which is deeply aware of the God-dimension of praxis, avoiding and/or enriching some modern reductive notions of praxis.[10] But there is much more that the saints can teach us too. Their attunement to praxis enabled them to develop profound explorations of human and ecclesial and social pathology, as we have noted. Because they didn't get lost in theory, they were profoundly aware of the shadow and night side of the human drama. They also often probed how one might translate spiritual and theological insights into ecclesial reforms. This is often the form that social transformation took among an Ignatius Loyola, Teresa of Avila, or John of the Cross.[11] In this sense the mystics might resensitize us to the institutional dimension of our religion. Of course, some have suggested, as we noted earlier, that we need to extend what the mystics have begun by probing the socio-political structures of society beyond the Church, and we need to do this in a more systemic manner. I would generally agree with this, but perhaps we need to consult much more vigorously some of the more contemporary martyrs and saints who are already on to much of this. Also, I would suggest that a more sustained "consultation" of the belief in the communion of saints might surface something of a sociopolitical punch in our tradition, much as the liberationist reading of Jesus' kingdom of God has already done.

4. The Saints as "Appropriate" and "Critical"

One way to sum up the hermeneutical contribution of consulting the saints as we have explored it in these pages is to view such a consultation as providing us with both an "appropriate" and a "critical" mediation of the Christian tradition. In general terms, we can say with many today that the theological enterprise is one of contributing toward the contemporary actualization of the Christian tradition. This actualization of the tradition involves a constant intersection between the heritage of the past (tradition in the sense of the "texts" of the past) and our ongoing contemporary experience/situation. This actualization is for the sake of the tradition, to keep it vital, contemporary. Theology attempts

various scholarly "mediations" of the tradition to our contemporary situation, if you will. An "appropriate" mediation
would be one which helps us articulate the Christian community's self-understanding as expressed in its great texts,
documents, and heritage in general. A "critical" mediation
would be one which attempts to correct inadequacies in the
community's self-understanding, precisely for the sake of the
community and its tradition. Expressed in a theological id-
iom, the Jesus Christ event requires of us that we be open
to a correction of our community self-understanding precisely if we are to remain faithful to it.

A theological consultation of the saints sometimes, possibly most often, aids us in developing a more "appropriate"
mediation of our Christian tradition. The saints, mystics, and
martyrs of either the past or the present intensively manifest
aspects of the community's inherited vision and praxis. At
times, this may appear to be simply an exemplification of
what is commonly taught in the community. Quite clearly
the theology of many of the saints and mystics simply echoes
the theology in possession at the time. But this is not without
its theological relevance, for the way the saints embody theology and the implications they draw can be enormously
fruitful for the theologian's task. Particularly in our experiential and praxis-oriented age, the saints aid us in developing an experiential and practical mediation of the "theology and doctrine in possession." A reading, for example, of
Loyola's *Spiritual Exercises* will reveal much that was commonly taught in the Church and theology of his time: the
sovereignty of God, the emerging sense of the Church, the
doctrine of sin and salvation, the typical afterlife beliefs, etc.
And what is true of Loyola is true of many saints: we meet
with the common heritage. But Loyola, like many of the
other mystics, quite personally and experientially probes
these beliefs and lives them out. Both the meaning and the

praxis of the common heritage often surfaces in striking and attractive ways.

At times, however, a consulting of the saints provides us with a more appropriate mediation of the tradition, not because the saints exemplify the "theology in possession," but because they experientially and practically rehabilitate dimensions of the tradition which remain ignored or underplayed. Or, if they do not "rehabilitate" such dimensions, they at least give them a prominence greater than they receive from the authorities in possession or from the faithful in general. At times the saints can seem very radical and even shocking simply because they are embodying something quite traditional. This is one of the ways in which the depth of their experience and the intensity of it enables them to transcend some of the ecclesial and wider cultural limitations of their times. Joann Wolski Conn's feminist reading of St. Thérèse of Lisieux can serve as a representative example of what I have in mind. Against the backdrop of nineteenth century French "official" theology and popular piety, Thérèse seems strikingly original. But her originality is one of recovering nearly lost elements of our biblical heritage: a God of tenderness in place of a God of rigorism and fear; a spirituality of daily life (the "little way") in place of an exaggerated search for "the more difficult"; a theology of a Church of love, rather than the ecclesiology of the Church as *societas perfecta,* with its exaggeration of the institutional and hierarchical aspects of a theology of the Church.[12]

I have tried to indicate earlier that there are enormous treasures of a theological sort awaiting the theologian who takes the saints seriously. Thérèse is only one example of how they can help us rehabilitate the richer texture of our tradition. In theology and anthropology, the saints can revitalize a biblical, more historical, and often panentheistic vision of God whose dwelling in our lives makes of us theomorphic

beings. In christology and soteriology, they can balance the
abstract Christ of Chalcedon and the imperial Christ of the
Constantinian settlement with the humiliated Jesus of the
Gospels, whose greatest concern is for the poor. And we
could continue on through ecclesiology to eschatology.
Hopefully our survey at this essay's beginning will now pack
a somewhat greater "punch." Might I recommend turning to
it anew to catch some idea of how the saints are powerful
theological allies in the quest for a mediation of the greater
richness of our tradition, in both its meaning and praxis dimensions.

Finally, it also seems clear that at times a theological
consultation of the saints can result in a correction of an
inadequacy of the tradition, or in the development of a new
insight or mode of behavior. This is what I am calling the
"critical" function of consulting the saints. It is perhaps the
most dramatic way in which the saints help us keep the tradition moving and intersecting with contemporary experience. As I indicated earlier, occasionally the saint's depth of
experience and sensitive openness to new experiences qualifies him or her for a discovery of a genuinely "new" aspect
of the Christian revelation. Karl Rahner, for example, was
convinced that Ignatius Loyola's elaboration of discernment
in the *Spiritual Exercises* was a genuinely new Christian discovery of the "modern individual subject": "The will of God
is not . . . simply and entirely transmitted through the objective structures of the world and the Church. The subject
goes beyond what is universally valid and seeks through his
choice his own unique truth, setting himself at a distance
(termed 'indifference') from every particular existing object."[13] Von Balthasar suggests that Adrienne von Speyr's experiential insights into Jesus' descent into hell may signal a
genuinely new understanding of the universalist implications
of salvation as a gift somehow reaching all: a kind of revi-

sionist apocatastasis theory might flow from this.[14] The feminist consultation of the saints and mystics is aiding us in discovering the rather massive misogynism that pollutes our tradition. This is in some ways a more "appropriate" mediation of our tradition, for it helps us recover a more liberated image of women. But it is also a genuinely new and critical correction of an inadequacy in our tradition. Is the existence of the martyrs in South America, in Africa, in Asia, in the persecuted lands of Russia, etc., also a stimulus to a genuinely new discovery of the systemic nature of social and possibly even ecclesial pathology? Will the emerging Christian consultation of the mystics of the venerable non-Christian religions possibly result in a mutation of some aspects of our theology: a heightened reunion between theology and spirituality, of course, but possibly also a new development in our understanding of the universality of revelation and salvation and of the uniqueness of Jesus' mediatorial role in history? This list is only suggestive. Again, I would recommend that the reader return to our survey at this essay's beginning for other possible *nova* contributed to theology by the saints, martyrs, and mystics.

Notes

[1]Egan, p. 382.

[2]Karl Rahner, "The Church of the Saints," *Theological Investigations* III (Baltimore: Helicon, 1967), pp. 91–104; "Why and How Can We Venerate the Saints?" and "All Saints," *Theological Investigations* VIII (New York: Herder and Herder, 1971), pp. 3–23, 24–29.

[3]See II/n. 4; Dante Germino, *Beyond Ideology: The Revival of Political Theory* (New York: Harper and Row, 1967), pp. 6 and 183, in explaining the thought of Eric Voegelin, is especially helpful on this widened notion of experience: "Human experience has

many levels, and it is no less real or factual for being inner experience instead of external observation or sensory response to a physical stimulus." If we restrict experience only to sense experience "other dimensions of experience, apprehended through the *nous* or eye of the mind instead of the eye of the physical body, are treated as subjective because they are not as universally shared and readily communicable as experiences on the level of physical sensation." Inward human experience requires "laborious formation of character," but it seems that the vast majority of people "are able without comparable effort to verify" propositions derived from sense experience. If we rely only upon the latter this would mean that "people of the meanest capacities" will be the determiners of what constitutes the true field of human experience.

[4]Meyendorff, *Byzantine Theology,* pp. 10, 8–9.

[5]Rahner, "The Church of the Saints," p. 100.

[6]Von Balthasar, *Thérèse of Lisieux,* pp. xv, xviii; Richard Woods, *Mysterion: An Approach to Mystical Spirituality* (Chicago: Thomas More, 1981), pp. 171, 165.

[7]Hans-Georg Gadamer, *Truth and Method* (New York: Seabury, 1975), p. 319.

[8]Egan, p. 383; I/n. 5; Von Balthasar, "Theology and Sanctity," pp. 51, 49, and *St. Thérèse of Lisieux,* p. xv. Karl Rahner, *I Remember* (New York: Crossroad, 1985), p. 96, offers this view: "The pope is the highest representative of the Church, and, if you like, of Catholic Christianity with respect to certain juridical, ecclesial structures. But I maintain that the most humble, the most loving (to put it in this old-fashioned way), the most holy, the most apparently obscure person in the Church, and not the pope, is at the top of the hierarchy, the real hierarchy for which the Church is only a means.

"In his *Divine Comedy,* Dante, who is recognized by the Church as a great Christian poet, placed certain popes who did not please him in hell. That may have actually been unfair, but the highest representative within the social fabric is not necessarily the highest representative of the real reason for which the Church exists. She is there so that God may be worshipped, praised, and loved, and so that people might love one another and be selfless, and for that the saints are the real representatives. Innocent III was pope, but Francis of Assisi was the highest in the only hierarchy that ultimately counts." Rahner is underscoring a theme which is well celebrated in theological and literary circles.

⁹*Dogmatic Constitution on the Church* 50, *The Documents of Vatican II,* Walter M. Abbott, ed. (New York: America Press, 1966), p. 82; cf. Otto Semmelroth, "The Eschatological Nature of the Pilgrim Church and Her Union with the Heavenly Church," in Herbert Vorgrimler, ed., *Commentary on the Documents of Vatican II,* I (New York: Herder and Herder, 1967), pp. 282–284. For the logic of eschatological statements, see Karl Rahner's classic essay, "The Hermeneutics of Eschatological Assertions," *Theological Investigations* IV, pp. 323–346.

¹⁰See my *The Jesus Debate,* pp. 36–38, and Kasper, "Theologie und Heiligkeit," pp. 12–16.

¹¹Egan, p. 163.

¹²I/n. 31.

¹³Karl Rahner, "Modern Piety and the Experience of Retreats," *Theological Investigations* XVI (New York: Seabury, 1979), pp. 135–155 at 141. Cf. his *Ignatius of Loyola* (London: Collins, 1979), which he wrote with the aid of Paul Imhof and Helmut Nils Loose, for a kind of practical modern adaptation of Loyola's originality.

¹⁴"Revisionist," in the sense that it is hopeful about the possibility of universal salvation; it does not dogmatically predict such a reality, nor does it deny human freedom. Cf. *The Von Balthasar Reader,* p. 422: "It is only permissible to say so much: God even as redeemer respects the freedom which God has bestowed upon his creature and with which it is capable of resisting his love. This respecting means that God does not overrule, pressure, or coerce with the omnipotence of his absolute freedom the precarious freedom of the creature. In doing so he would contradict himself. It remains however to consider whether God is not free to encounter the sinner turned away from him in the form of weakness of the crucified brother abandoned by God, and indeed in such a way

that it becomes clear to the one turned away: this (like me) God-forsaken one is so for my sake. In this situation one can no longer speak of any overpowering if, to the one who has chosen (maybe one should say: thinks he has chosen) the complete loneliness of being-only-for-oneself, God himself enters into his very loneliness as someone who is even more lonely. To get an insight into this one must recall what was said at the start according to which the world with all its destinies of freedom has been founded antici-patorily in the mystery of the sacrificed Son of God: this descent is a priori deeper than that to which one lost in the world can attain. Even what we call 'hell' is, although it is the place of des-olation, always still a christological place." Also cf. p. 403: "To the central insights bestowed on her [i.e., Adrienne von Speyr] belong the mysteries of Holy Saturday and hence of hell and of universal redemption as well."

V

A Few Remaining Issues

I hope the reader will have found this work's basic line of argumentation to be plausible. But even if that be the case, I would like to underscore the introductory and even tentative nature of this study. Much that has been only suggested here needs and deserves more sustained thought. And I look forward to helpful yet critical observations from my colleagues.

Before passing to the latter part of this book, in which I will actually engage in a theological consultation of some of the saints by way of exemplification of this work's thesis, let me surface a few further issues needing consideration. One that immediately comes to mind is the limited value of the consultation of the saints. If we view theology as the attempt at a conversation—an "attempt," because at times it breaks down—between the tradition and our contemporary experience, then a consultation of the saints has a modest role to play in this project. The saints do not constitute the totality of the tradition or our contemporary experience. The Scriptures are, of course, a key source—for most, the normative source, requiring of theologians basic continuity with its revelation. Additionally most of us would recognize some kind of ecclesial authority (or magisterium), the liturgy, the arts, and whatever else might be a source of God's self-communication. In other words, the norm of theology cannot be the isolated experiences and teachings of a few, but only God's truth and praxis as it is disclosed to us through the entire sweep of the tradition actualized anew in each age.

Only if we use the term "saints" in its widest possible sense of embracing all the faithful of all the ages can we see it as a more total norm of theology. But usually we consult, not all the faithful, but various representatives from among them which seem to stand out.

I think it would be a mistake to isolate the varied saints out, setting them up as a kind of norm over other usually accepted norms in theology. It's not a question of *either* the saints *or* Scripture *or* dogma and magisterium *or* other faithful members of the Church. Such an either-or approach would be very unfaithful to the saints themselves, for their lives and teaching reflect, are informed by, and are meant to enrich the Church itself in all its aspects. And, of course, God's self-communication can't be limited to the saints, mystics, or martyrs a particular theologian might choose to consult. A theological consultation of the saints simply has to recognize its limits, lest it become a new form of elitist theological totalitarianism.

A second and very crucial concern is that of the need for a "critical appropriation" of the saints by the theologian. I suspect that some theologians won't allow the saints—or mystics, or martyrs—into their theological imaginations precisely because oftentimes those saints seem uncritical in their thought and sometimes bizarre in their praxis. I think there's no disputing these latter points. But I don't think that should lead us to ignore the saints. Rather, it seems to heighten the need for some mode of critical appropriation of them.

My own suggestion at this point is that we need to learn to apply our theological hermeneutics to the saints, just as we have learned to apply it to the Scriptures, and are learning to apply it to the fathers, the magisterium, the liturgy, etc. Let me hazard a few suggestions here, based upon my own reading of developments in theological hermeneutics. Let me begin with a model of theology which I believe many, perhaps most, centrist theologians would accept; namely, theology is a critical engagement between the tradition and our contemporary experience. The task of the theologian is to try to help actualize the meaning and truth of the Christian tradition for each age. Only in this way can the tradition really remain alive and contemporary. Now a theological consultation of the saints is in the service of this larger theological project: the experiences and expressions of the saints, the mystics, and the martyrs are a part of both the tradition and our contemporary experience. The theologian needs to grow accustomed to thinking about the tradition and contemporary experience in these terms.

Secondly, a growing number of theologians suggest that we can gain a better understanding of what this critical engagement between tradition and contemporary experience means by employing the model of a "conversation." A genuine conversation, in distinction to talking past one another, is a back and forth, genuinely to-and-fro movement between the conversation partners. Plato's dialogues are a superb example of what we mean. The heart and key to a successful conversation is to allow oneself to be open to the truth or the subject matter, come what may. This means we have to listen, be open to correction and expansion, and in general move beyond our initial biases and hunches. The conversation always breaks down when we cease being open to the subject matter.

So, the theologian tries to converse with the tradition. That means, he or she tries to be open to the truth or subject matter—the theologian might more commonly say "revelation"—expressed in varied ways in the past and present. Both the tradition and our contemporary experience "participate" in and express in varying ways that "truth." Coming to our theme, our aim is to open ourselves to the revelatory disclosure expressed in varied ways by the saints of past and present. That is what it means to converse theologically with the saints.

But how might we relatively insure that we're genuinely conversing, genuinely engaging in that to-and-fro dialogue between tradition and contemporary experience? How can we keep the conversation from complete breakdown? At this point I would recommend that we take a clue from the hermeneutical thought of the philosopher Paul Ricoeur.[1] He suggests that our to-and-fro conversational movement might move through three distinct but interrelated moments: (1) understanding, (2) explanation, and (3) comprehension. This is Ricoeur's own modulation of the traditional philosophical distinction between *verstehen* (understanding) and *erklären* (explanation). All of us begin our conversation with the saints—or enter into the engagement betwen tradition and contemporary experience—with our initial formation: our basic beliefs and practices, concerns, questions, hopes and fears, our "horizon" of understanding and action. Now this initial formation constitutes our "understanding." It is through this that we approach the conversation and are able to even enter into it. Understanding is our anticipatory ability to be open to and appropriate the truth or subject matter of the conversation.

But we can refine our understanding, and should. Our anticipatory understanding is only a first guess or hunch, if you will, of what's going forward in the theological conversation. Now this attempt to refine is what Ricoeur means by "explanation." The latter is not a simple application of a recipe. "There are no rules for making good guesses," says Ricoeur.[2] This means that our understanding always informs our explaining. But granted this, explanation is an attempt to be more methodic and critical. It's a way of moving toward ever more probable interpretations of the "subject matter" of the conversation.

What Ricoeur means is that theology has available to it varied methods which have been found highly useful for the theological task. Ricoeur is especially sensitive to the literary methods which are available. Oftentimes the tradition takes a "textual" form: revelation reaches us by way of images and symbols that have been structured into various genres; for example, myths, narratives, psalms, prayers, apocalypses, sayings, etc. Ricoeur knows that Christian revelation can't be reduced to a written text. But that revelation finds itself mediated to us in some form of expression (a "text" in this wider sense).[3] Literary methods can aid us in paying attention to the images/symbols and genres, helping us unlock how and what they're trying to disclose. So a consultation of the saints can learn through literary methods to grow sensitive to the "media" through which the saints have expressed themselves. As we will see, the saints often favor the narrative genre, since they do their theology in a kind of autobiographical manner. But they are also quite capable of exalted poetry and even art, and the use of highly complex symbols. Literary methods can aid us in refining our ability to understand these varied media and what they do.

But the lived expressions (texts) of the saints also raise historical and theological issues. Ricoeur likes to say that the text "opens up a world" before us. A "world" of historical and/or theological reality is opened up in front of the text.[4] Literary methods of analysis can be helpful at refining our ability to penetrate this "world," but other methods have also been found helpful. We can think of the long and sophisticated use of historical methods of analysis in Bible studies and theology, and the use of varied philosophical methods of analysis. Now other methods are coming into greater prominence too, like psychological and sociopolitical ones, which enable us to surface the psychosocial dimensions of religion. All of these, needless to say, can be helpful to the

theologian as she or he engages in a consultation of the
saints. The use of these methods promotes a kind of "conflict
of interpretations," to cite Ricoeur again.[5] Still, by appealing
to literary, historical, psychosocial, and philosophical-theo-
logical warrants, the theologian insures a healthy critical
spirit in the attempt to appropriate the saints. If you will,
these varied explanatory methods keep us from letting the
theological conversation break down through a simple capit-
ulation to our own biases and/or fears. All of this leads, finally, to "comprehension." As we allow ourselves to be transformed in thought and practice through the conversation, we
are "com-prehended," as it were, changed and enriched.

Hans-Georg Gadamer will call the comprehension moment of the conversation a "fusion of horizons." As we participate in the to-and-fro movement of the conversation, we
find ourselves undergoing a kind of conversion. Gadamer's
own term for it is *Horizontverschmeltzung*, which one interpreter translates as a "wiping away of horizons" rather than
a "fusion of horizons."[6] To the degree that this occurs, in the
critical way made possible by the explanatory moment, one
can say that he or she has been truly open to the revelatory
disclosure provided by the saints.

I would suggest that some such hermeneutics as this is
crucial for our task. It keeps us genuinely open to the saints
in a disciplined manner. And yet it enables us to discrimi-
nate. A theology which wants to consult the saints isn't com-
mitted to swallowing anything and everything a particular
saint, mystic, or martyr might have expressed in some manner. The theologian will be attracted to varied expressions
of the saints, to be sure. But the theologian will need to
bring forth warrants of varied kind—literary, historical, psychosocial, philosophical—to make the case for the validity of
the particular "attraction." I will try to do precisely this in
the representative consultations of the saints to follow. Put-

ting this hermeneutics to work within the context of this book will probably be the best way to make the case for our approach.

A last issue I would mention is the question of how someone might practically begin a consultation of the saints. How might we actually get the conversation started? Every conversation is selective; we don't talk with everybody. So, too, is our possible conversation with the saints. We will inevitably be selective. But I suggest that we try to be critically selective. Our entire cultural and theological formation will likely guide us, if we allow it to. Perhaps our current and/or continual theological interests and passions will lead us to certain saints. I personally found myself attracted to Gregory Palamas and Teresa of Avila because I'm deeply interested in the experiential foundations of theology. Teresa has also been very helpful for my work in christology. Might I also suggest that we consider consulting those we might consider the living saints and mystics? Von Balthasar wasn't afraid to consult Von Speyr, for example. Nor were Evelyn Underhill, Abbot Cuthbert Butler, and Lutheran Archbishop Söderblom afraid to consult the mystic Friedrich von Hügel. Nor are the Russian Orthodox hesitant to consult their Fathers Gleb Yakunin and Dmitri Dudko. In any case, after we have "selected" one or several possible candidates, I have found it helpful to stay with them, reading them as thoroughly as possible (or speaking with them as the case may be). I try to make it my constant practice to consult them on every theological project I engage in. This sensitizes one to this kind of consultation, and eventually leads to an interest in and exploration of others from our rich hagiographical tradition. It is a process of widening our theological imaginations, a kind of habituation exercise.

Let me end this chapter with a comment from Umberto Eco's engaging *The Name of the Rose*. The comment is made by the character Adso as he tries to describe his companion and teacher William, and it expresses something of the possible enrichment awaiting the theologian if she or he will consult the saints: ". . . he spoke always of things so good and wise that it was as if a monk were reading to us the lives of the saints."[7]

Notes

[1]Cf. Particularly Paul Ricoeur, *Interpretation Theory: Discourse and the Surplus of Meaning* (Fort Worth, Texas: Texas Christian University, 1976). Quite helpful in this regard are John W. Van Den Hengel, *The Home of Meaning: The Hermeneutics of the Subject of Paul Ricoeur* (Washington, D. C.: University Press of America, 1982), and David Tracy, *The Analogical Imagination* as well as his *Blessed Rage for Order*. I've tried to present my own summary and evaluation of hermeneutics in my *The Jesus Debate*, esp. pp. 45-89.

[2]*Ibid.*, p. 76.

[3]Cf. Paul Ricoeur, "The Model of the Text: Meaningful Action Considered as a Text," in his *Hermeneutics and the Human Sciences*, J. B. Thompson, ed. (New York: Cambridge University, 1981), pp. 197-221.

[4]*Interpretation Theory*, p. 94, for example.

[5]Cf. Paul Ricoeur, *The Conflict of Interpretations: Essays in Hermeneutics*, Don Ihde, ed. (Evanston: Northwestern University, 1974).

[6]Hans-Georg Gadamer, *Truth and Method* (New York: Seabury, 1975), *passim;* Van Den Hengel, p. 199.

[7]Umberto Eco, *The Name of the Rose* (New York: Warner Books, 1984), p. 23. I might add that the hermeneutical approach to the saints recommended here comprehends the classical *trivium* of the true, the good, and the beautiful; that is, through the me-

dium of expression, appropriated through literary-aesthetic methods (beauty), truth and praxis (the good) are communicated to us and appropriated through varied methods of analysis.

VI

The Dark Night: A Theological Consultation

U p to this point this little study has tried to make the
case for the rich, theological suggestiveness of the
saints, the mystics, and the martyrs. In doing so, we have
tried to surface the variety of possible insights. But now it
is time to exemplify a theological consultation of the saints
in a more sustained way. And I have chosen as my first example the mystical theme of the dark night. We have already
seen hints of the fruitful possibilities latent in our theme.
Von Balthasar has written of the mystical dark night as a
possible source for the deepened understanding of the passion of Jesus. And to some extent he has pursued this theme
in his writings. Harvey Egan has explored, as well, how the
Church needs to undergo a collective dark night of purification to remain true to itself. And practical theologians are
beginning to surface the building blocks for a possible Christian analysis of pathology present in our theme.[1] The theme
of the dark night offers us an interesting intersection between speculative and practical theology. As we shall see, it
also seems to cut across most of the great themes of theology.
Because of this, theologians in differing specializations may
be able to sense something of the powerful impact a consultation of the saints might have in their areas of concentration. The theme also seems to possess a certain conge-
niality with our times. For is not our age a rather stressful,
dark moment in the history of the globe? A darkness which
is promising, to be sure, but surely painfully searing too?

Let me begin with some observations on the literary form of discourse about the "dark night." These observations are prompted by the insight of literary criticism that we should pay particular attention to the *form* of discourse we are considering. That form may not be merely a tool of communication, easily replaced by another form. It may be an essential dimension of the message: in some way, the message can communicate only through a particular literary form. Form and message are united in a kind of perichoresis very often. To move toward the latter we must dwell with the former. Paraphrasing Paul Ricoeur, if we begin with the literary form we are following the natural movement of interpretation: from the sense encoded in the form to the possible references opened up to us in front of the form.[2]

I will use a form of genre analysis suggested by both David Tracy and Paul Ricoeur as a tentative way of opening up our discussion. Let us entertain Ricoeur's suggestion that genres are not simply devices of classification but productive devices which actually generate insight. Keeping this in mind, we can see why he would say "that the confession of faith expressed in the biblical documents is directly modulated by the forms of discourse wherein it is expressed."[3] So I will propose that the religious disclosure expressed in dark night discourse is "directly modulated by the forms of discourse wherein it is expressed." I will try to be suggestive rather than exhaustive, highlighting some representative forms of dark night discourse.

A first and common genre to be considered is simply the *symbolism* of the "dark night" itself (together with its equivalents: "darkness," "cloud of unknowing," "nothingness," etc.). A "dark night" is not a concept in a descriptive kind of sense. In fact, like all truly religious symbols, this one abolishes the notion that one can pictorially describe the Divine. All religious symbolism abolishes language's ordinary referential function by opening us to a world which transcends sense description. But the symbolism of the dark night does this with a vengeance, if I can put it that way. The double negation of darkness and night negates any human pretensions to knowledge and thus intensifies the sense that we are confronting what transcends ordinary human description. In other words, the dark night is a symbolic form characterized by negation and intensification. It highlights the divine transcendence, its beyondedness, together with our inability to domesticate it. It brings front and center our inadequacy, perhaps also our sinfulness. It sensitizes us anew to the night side and shadow side of our existence, both individually and collectively.

So far as I can tell, different mystics who have either written or spoken of the dark night experience bring out varied dimensions of this multidimensional symbolism. Gregory of Nyssa, in his *The Life of Moses,* seems to highlight the divine transcendence:

> What does it mean that Moses entered the darkness and then saw God in it?
> . . . this is the seeing that consists in not seeing, because that which is sought transcends all knowledge, being separated on all sides by incomprehensibility as by a kind of darkness.

Or perhaps most readers will be familiar with the same insight in the later *The Mystical Theology* of Dionysius the Areopagite:

> Unto this Darkness which is beyond Light we pray that we may come, and may attain unto vision through the loss of sight and knowledge, and that in ceasing thus to see or know we may learn to know that which is beyond all perception and

understanding (for this emptying of our faculties
is true sight and knowledge), and that we may offer Him that transcends all things the praises of a
transcendent hymnody, which we shall do by
denying or removing all things that are—like as
men who, carving a statue out of marble, remove
all the impediments that hinder the clear percep-
tive of the latent image and by this mere removal
display the hidden statue itself in its hidden
beauty.

The correlative of divine transcendence is human fi-
niteness and a sense of our limits. Gregory of Nyssa, perhaps
alone of all the *patres*, has given the most intensive expression to this: "Since, then, those who know what is good by
nature desire participation in it, and since this good has no
limit, the participant's desire itself necessarily has no stop-
ping place but stretches out with the limitless." But the dark
night symbolism releases more than a sense of human finitude. It often intensifies our sense of sin, both individually
and collectively. We can be finite without being sinful. Although many of the great mystics through the ages have intensively experienced this dimension of our symbolism, few
have expressed it more pointedly than Thomas Merton in
what Harvey Egan helpfully calls Merton's "crisis mysticism":

The experience of "dread," "nothingness" and
"night" in the heart of man is then the awareness
of infidelity to the truth of our life. More, it is an
awareness of infidelity as unrepented and without
grace as *unrepentable*. It is the deep, confused,
metaphysical awareness of a *basic antagonism between the self and God* due to estrangement from

him by perverse attachment to a "self" which is
mysterious and illusory.

Merton seems to have known the collective dimensions
of the dark night too. But South American liberation theology seems particularly sensitive to it; says Gustavo Gutierrez,

> The passage through what has been called "the
> dark night" of injustice is part of the spiritual
> journey in Latin America. On this journey "of an
> entire people toward its liberation through the
> desert of structural and organized injustice that
> surrounds us . . . it is very important to perse-
> vere in prayer, even if we hardly do more than
> stammer groans and cries, while in this struggle
> the image of God in us is purified in an extraor-
> dinary 'dark night.' "

Divine transcendence, human finitude with its unending
searching, human sinfulness and societal oppression—these
are but representative dimensions of the powerful revelation
disclosed through the negations and intensifications of the
symbolism of the dark night.[4]

A second genre we might pursue is what I would call
dark night *poetry*. Perhaps this is another form of what Ricoeur would consider "hymnic supplication discourse" or
what we might call "desolatory poetry."[5] Of course I have in
mind Dante's *Inferno* and *Purgatorio*, but more especially
John of the Cross' great poem *Noche Oscura* and perhaps
even sections of *The Spiritual Canticle* and *The Living Flame
of Love*. Teresa of Avila has her great dark night poetry too:

> Dark is this existence;
> Bitter is its thrall:

Life that's lived without Thee
Is not life at all.
Oh, my sweetest Lover,
Miserable am I,
And my yearning for Thee
Makes me long to die.[6]

Like all poetry, this kind again abolishes the world of ordinary sense experience and opens us to a world which transcends ordinary description. And the use of the dark night symbolism again, through intensification and negation, heightens our experience of this transcendent world. But poetry introduces a new modulation into our symbolism. On the one hand it intensifies the intensification and negation of dark night symbolism, if I can put it this way. And it does this through its repetitions of our dark night theme, as well as through parallel symbolisms surfacing various dimensions of the dark night. The repetitions dull, numb, and "blind" the reader/hearer, should the poetry seek to surface the pain of the night, as in Teresa's poetry. In St. John's *Noche Oscura* the repetitive numbness seems to still the wandering mind, freeing it for the Beloved:

On that glad night,
In secret, for no one saw me,
Nor did I look at anything,
With no other light or guide
Than the one that burned in my heart . . .[7]

On the other hand, the integration of our dark night symbolism into the poem often transforms it into part of a larger dialogue. In this way, the poem surfaces how the dark night is a part of a movement toward a deepened communion with the Divine. In the *Noche Oscura* this remains somewhat obscure (fittingly for a night which is *oscura*), for the Divine Beloved is spoken of in the third person only:

I abandoned and forgot myself,
Laying my face on my Beloved . . .

But in *The Spiritual Canticle* and *The Living Flame of Love*
the dialogue with the Divine Thou erupts with full force
through the second person usage:

How gently and lovingly
You wake in my heart,
Where in secret You dwell alone;
And by your sweet breathing,
Filled with good and glory,
How tenderly you swell my heart with love![8]

The chanted, supplicatory nature of the poetry also intensifies the experience of being in dialogue with the Divine
Thou. Jean Baruzi suggests that John of the Cross' poem-
commentary form also gives expression to a kind of dialogue-
answer experience in the mystic. If you will, the Sanjuanist
commentary intensifies the mystic's own experience of dial-
ogical response to the divine summons.[9] In these ways, the
poetry brings out how the dark night experience is a truly
religious experience, an encounter with God, and not an experience of meaningless emptiness.

Finally, let me mention what I might call the dark night
narrative genre, or possibly *sub-narrative*, since this genre
usually forms a part of a larger narrative piece. I think this
was a favorite of Thomas Merton's: who could miss the jour-
nal-like, narrative quality of *The Seven Storey Mountain, The
Sign of Jonas, The Secular Journal of Thomas Merton, Con-
jectures of a Guilty Bystander,* and the *Asian Journal?* We
also find this sub-narrative in St. Teresa of Avila's autobiography. In the earlier part, the important chapters five and
six, she recounts her illnesses as a kind of purgative experience, and even refers to Job's experience as a paradigm of

her own. But it is in the great chapter thirty-two that she recounts her experience of hell, pointing out the correlation between dark night and hell in a classic way. ". . . I had seemingly been put in hell . . . here it is the soul itself that tears itself in pieces. . . . There was no light, but all was enveloped in the blackest darkness."[10] And who can forget the great manuscript "C" of St. Thérèse of Lisieux' biography, her great trial of faith: "He permitted my soul to be invaded by the thickest darkness, and that the thought of heaven, up until then so sweet to me, be no longer anything but the cause of struggle and torment."[11]

It is no accident that the dark night experience seeks its expression in the narrative form. As Ricoeur and Tracy have helpfully suggested, the *lived* quality of life seems to demand the narrative form.[12] For the narrative form brings out the movement or temporality of our lives, from beginning through middle to ending. If you will, the flow of existence finds expression in the narrated story. Also, the really lived tension and struggle, the pain and suspense, the darkness and light—all find expression in the narrative. In these ways, the narrative introduces its own modulations into the dark night symbolism. It intensifies the flow or temporality of the dark night, prolonging our experience of it, making us stay with it and endure it. Through the story we somehow experience the real tension of the darkness: we too are suspended in darkness. Like other narratives, these dark night stories bear a similarity-in-difference to our own. The bumpy, painful journey of the story is sufficiently like our own journey that we can identify with the mystic's dark night. Yet the mystic's journey is sufficiently different, so that it stimulates our curiosity and openness. The narrative, if you will, somehow opens us to the dark night, leads us into it. If the dark night poetry perhaps tends to stress how the experience of darkness is an elevated experience of the few, the dark night narrative might democratize the experience. And again the narrative, by integrating the dark night into the story of the mystical ascent to divine union and joy, brings out, like the poetry, the revelatory nature of this suffering.

Might I suggest that the reader try to familiarize herself or himself with examples of each of these dark night genres? Meditatively dwelling in turn with each of these forms of dark night discourse could be the best way to begin a theological consultation of the mystical dark night. In this way, to paraphrase Ricoeur, we allow the form itself to open us to the possible world of disclosure in the dark night. Or, again to return to Ricoeur, we move naturally from the sense of the genre to the theological references it opens up before us. Buttressed, now, with a first sensitivity to the rich levels of meaning found in the mystic's dark night—divine transcendence, human finitude, individual and collective pathology—let us continue our theological consultation by probing what the dark night might disclose about some of the great themes of Christian theology.

Anthropology is probably a good place to begin, since the mystic's experience is commonly understood as a paradigm of the Christian understanding of human experience in general. Here I would suggest that the dark night experience serves primarily a corrective function in the theological formulation of anthropology. It keeps our anthropology modest and humble, by reminding us of the incomplete nature of human existence. For, as Gregory of Nyssa particularly points out, the correlative of an Unlimited Mystery is an unending quest by the finite creature. In some ways this is a theme dear to our historically conscious epoch, with its emphasis upon our conditionedness and temporality. But the dark night experience goes beyond this to highlight the morally ambiguous and sinful nature of human existence too. In this sense, it keeps our anthropology critical, promoting a sense of suspicion of overly optimistic and utopian versions of anthropology. Our night side is our sinful self, in both its individual and collective forms of embodiment. Thomas Merton's "dread" and "night" highlights the one for us, and Gustavo Gutierrez' "dark night of injustice" focuses the other. Thus, the dark night emphasizes for us a fundamental truth pointed out by the Second Vatican Council: "The call to grandeur and the depths of misery are both a part of human experience."[13] If you will, the mystical darkness intensifies our awareness of the latter part of this statement. It brings what some theologians call "negative experiences" into a certain theological prominence, forcing us to do at least some of our theologizing from them.

An anthropology modified by the dark night experience has a particular message for an age influenced by the western experience of the Enlightenment. The reduction of reality to sense experience, the erosion of the sense of Mystery in its positive sense as an indication of humanity's openness to an Unlimited and Divine Horizon[14]—these notions meet with their critique in the dark night of unknowing, which reminds us experientially of our unlimited aspiration. We now know, too, that some forms of theology have failed to allow themselves to be critiqued by the dark night experience. They have given birth to an excessively rationalistic and propositional understanding of divine revelation, which claims to know more than it really does and perhaps was more influenced by the rationalistic trends of the early Enlightenment than it cares to admit. Some forms of contemporary "atheism" may be a reaction to this arrogant style of theology, for, if you will, atheism would seem to exaggerate the transcendence of the Divine. The dark night experience does not exaggerate, but it does intensify, the divine transcendence. In this regard, such rationalistic theologies would do well to "reappropriate" these explosive lines from Gregory of Nyssa's *Life of Moses*, the work that is the great grandfather of the dark night experience:

> This truly is the vision of God: never to be satisfied in the desire to see him. But one must always, by looking at what he can see, rekindle his desire to see more. Thus, no limit would interrupt growth in the ascent to God, since no limit to the Good can be found nor is the increasing of desire for the Good brought to an end because it is satisfied.[15]

An anthropology that keeps in touch with the dark night experience, especially some of the more contemporary modulations of that night, will also be able to appropriate somewhat more critically the lessons of the so called second or late Enlightenment, so emphasized by all forms of sociopolitical theology. As we remember, this "later" Enlightenment was critical of the naivete and optimism of the first. Unlike the first Enlightenment, which stressed the emancipatory power of a liberated human reason, this later one stressed the irrational, passional, dark side of human existence. It also stressed the social and institutional manifestations of irrationality. It was aware that the great experiment of the first Enlightenment, namely, the French Revolution, had derailed into a bloody reign of terror and a dictatorship. Humans were governed by more than reason. There is, in other words, a conflictual aspect to human anthropology. The development of reason must go along with a struggle against the irrational tendencies of the human psyche (the beloved study of psychoanalysis) and the institutionalized forms of human violence (the beloved study of critical sociologies).

A Christian anthropology, informed by the dark night, also realizes this conflictual aspect of human existence. Human life is not a serene process of ever greater movement toward God and neighborly love, as some overly utopian brands of Christian anthropology lead one to believe. Human growth is a struggle against the urge not to grow, but to fixate. There seems to be this "antagonism between the self and God" which Merton was the master at detecting, an antagonism which truly darkened our experience. Perhaps our experience of the late Enlightenment has reawakened our awareness of this side of the dark night experience. But the mystics didn't need to wait for the second Enlightenment. For a further correlate of the experience of divine transcendence is a concomitant experience of our own dark side. This is why entrance into the "cloud of unknowing" brings with it "a strong, deep, interior sorrow," according to the author of the great classic by that name. Or, as John of the Cross puts it, "The first and chief benefit that this dry and dark night of contemplation causes is the knowledge of self and of one's own misery."[16]

There is a sociopolitical edge to a conflictual anthropology too. We have already seen Gustavo Gutierrez, the "father" of liberation theology, speak of the "dark night of injustice." Certainly it is the liberation theologians who have done most to reawaken us to the sociopolitical edge of the dark night: ". . . the classic spiritual combat is making more searching demands because it has taken on social and historical dimensions," says Gutierrez of the poor in South America.[17] This is an insight continuous with our entire tradition. Jesus was aware that the entrance of his kingdom into history would bring with it a dark night of conflict with the ruling powers of his time:

> Nation will rise against nation, one kingdom
> against another. . . . They will hand you over to
> the courts. . . . You will be arraigned before gov-

ernors and kings on my account and have to tes-
tify to your faith before them.

During that period after trials of every sort *the
sun will be darkened, the moon will not shed its
light*, stars will fall out of the skies, and the heavenly hosts will be shaken. Then men will see the
Son of Man coming in the clouds with great
power and glory (Mk 13:8-9, 24-26, my italics).

Liberation theology, then, seems to be reawakening us to an
old theme in the tradition; namely, that the Christian life
involves an active commitment to a struggle on behalf of the
justice, love, and peace of Jesus' kingdom of God. In our
time and culture, there is a particular need to bring this facet
out. For we have a tendency to stress love as the highest
ideal of the Christian life, but all too often "love" means
personal and interpersonal manifestations of love. Bourgeois
and eros-dominated models of love tend to reign in our culture. It's probably not enough to say that the Christian is
called to live out an anthropology of love. We must add: and
of justice, involving us in an active struggle against all forms
of injustice.

I indicated earlier, but only in passing, that attentiveness to our mystical dark night tradition would enable us to
reappropriate the concerns of the later Enlightenment in a
more critical manner. Let me pursue this thought a bit more
at this point. By "more critically" I mean in a way which
avoids some of the limitations of the psychoanalytic and critical social sciences stemming from the late Enlightenment.
But to phrase this more positively and perhaps less insularly,
the mystical dark night enables us to incorporate the concerns of the late Enlightenment into our theology in our own
Christian way. Like the late Enlightenment, we Christians
want to be attentive to the shadow and night side of human

existence: the irrational, the passional, the violent, the sinful. But as Segundo Galilea put it, "A sense of sin is more than a sense of what is good or bad."[18] Here Galilea is pointing to the peculiarly Christian twist which our tradition gives to the uncovering of evil in history. The mystical dark night of the awareness of human pathology stems from an awareness of God's ever greater love and sensitivity toward us. As we have said, it is the correlate of God's transcendent love. In some ways this heightens our outrage at evil. And yet the outrage does not cripple us or eat away at us, for there is the awareness, albeit dark, of the supporting ground of a Divine Companion. As *The Cloud of Unknowing* puts it, "Were he [i.e., the mystic] not somehow nourished by the consolation of contemplative prayer, a man would be completely crushed by the knowing and feeling of his being."[19]

Speaking of the specifically Christian dimension of the dark night experience is an appropriate place to approach the christological implications of our theme. What light might the mystical dark night cast upon the mystery of Jesus Christ? Again I would suggest that the dark night performs a corrective function in christology (and soteriology), helping us to attend to the "dark" or "shadow" side of the explosion of the Jesus event. Let me introduce what I mean with the aid of St. Thérèse of Lisieux, perhaps to some an "unlikely" source of christological wisdom, but then the Jesus event is rather "unlikely" in terms of the usually prevailing standards of the world. In her *Story of a Soul,* she speaks from time to time of entering into dark nights, but in her last year of life she apparently endured a great "trial of faith." The subnarrative portion of her narrative in which she speaks of this trial is a classic example of the narrative-genre's ability to thrust the reader into the flow and duration of the turbulent ups and downs of the dark night experience.

Thérèse tells us that "the timid glimmerings of the dawn

have given way to the burning heat of noon." Her soul is "invaded by the thickest darkness." The very thought of heaven causes her only "struggle and torment." It is as if she were "in a country which is covered in thick fog." Her "heart fatigued by the darkness which surrounds it" enters into "the night of nothingness." But she indicates that this is a theologically rich night: "God was enlightening my soul" and "He was giving me even the experience of *years*." For through this dark experience she seems finally to gain understanding of the center of the Christian faith: the Jesus event. Thérèse expresses herself unsystematically, as the insights come to her in the flow of her narrative. But taken as a whole, these insights add up to a profound comprehension of the mystery of christology and soteriology. In this sense, her dark night experience is paradigmatic of the ability of the dark night to teach us christological truths.

In her narrative, Thérèse builds up a correlation between God, Jesus, and herself and other humans. There seems to be an oscillation between these three, such that an insight into one member of this "trinity" produces an insight into the other. She begins by saying that "those souls are rare who don't measure the divine power according to their own narrow minds; people want exceptions everywhere on earth, but God alone hasn't the right to make any exceptions!" Here she indicates that her dark night experience is pointing up the night side of our human insight into God: our desire to measure the divine by our standards. The arrogance of our God-thinking is now breaking down in the night: the divine "Moreness" is now reasserting itself experientially. But this is linked with a new experience of Jesus. Somehow the unexpected insight into God comes from an unexpected insight into Jesus: "Never have I felt before this . . . how sweet and merciful the Lord really is. . . ." She adds that "God has given me the grace to understand what charity is," and then points out that now she grasps the meaning of the great love commands of Jesus (cf. Mt 22:39 and Jn 13:34-35). The Jesus event is a mystery of love, and this new insight causes an eruption in her own life and the lives of those she can somehow touch. Her only desire now is that of "loving to the point of dying love." She wants, like Jesus, to "be broken through love." In this way her own martyrdom can become "the martyrdom of all." She now only seems to think of others and so "she begs pardon for her brothers." It is as if the dark night has revealed to her the "broken" and therefore utterly self-less nature of Jesus' love. Before this experience, her love was rather more self-focused and less costly. She had first to undergo what she called the "exile of the heart" before she could learn that a properly Jesus-oriented love is one which "expands" the soul completely beyond itself.[20]

In other words, Thérèse's dark night has aided her in thinking of christology and soteriology as primarily a mystery of love. Hers is a love christology, whose "center," in the words of the International (Papal) Theological Commission, "is a metaphysic of charity" leading us "to participate in building a *civilization of love* in human history."[21] But it is important to note the specific contribution of the dark night experience in this love christology. The danger of a love christology in a culture like our own (which by the way is not too different from the pampered, bourgeois life which Thérèse lived) is that we will too easily domesticate the kind of love which is expressed in the Jesus event. We naturally derive our understanding of love from the region of familial and interpersonal-intimate relationships. But the dark night stretched Thérèse beyond this domestication of love. She learned something of the *broken* and even martyrdom-producing love of Jesus which stretched him out beyond himself and his intimates to all, unknown, unintimate, unwanted, and even sinners. What flows through Jesus, making of him the Christ, is a divine mystery of utterly selfless charity. This is why there is a soteriological edge to the Jesus event: the very nature of selfless charity is to reach out beyond itself to those in need. As is well known, this took the form, in Thérèse, herself a cloistered Carmelite nun, of a special sensitivity for the missions, finally being proclaimed by Pope Pius XI in 1927 a patroness of all missionaries, equal in status to St. Francis Xavier.

If we follow Thérèse's clue, the mystical dark night, at least on one of its levels, is a plunge into the ocean of radically selfless love. The darkness or night dimension seems to be the annihilation of our ego (our self in that sense). If we do our christology and soteriology from this basis, we seem to confront the kind of love God is trying to reveal to us in the Jesus event. This provides us with an insight into the link between christology and soteriology. The Jesus event saves, not because God somehow extrinsically decides to credit Jesus with the earning of humanity's salvation, but because the mystery of a divine and selfless love flows out through Jesus into history. In this way, we are better able to grasp the intrinsic connection between christology and soteriology. But this dark night experience is also a corrective to all kinds of christological developments in our tradition, as distinct from soteriology, if I may put it that way. A love christology, as illustrated in Thérèse, could balance the more abstract christologies of the great councils (Nicaea and Chalcedon), which dwell rather abstractly upon the inner constitution of Jesus as the Christ. These "conciliar" christologies are not wrong, but they need balancing by the kind of insights flowing from the mystic's experiences. The dark night of love links us, perhaps, a bit more powerfully with the biblical Jesus of love. Also corrected is any tendency to "imperialize" Jesus into a kind of cosmic monarch, distant and untouched by Thérèse's sense of God's merciful love. The Christ of the Constantinian settlement, who was perhaps too much of an imperial Lord made in the image and likeness of the emperor, needs the purification of our dark night. Interestingly, too, I think a love christology along the lines suggested by Thérèse could aid a christology in not giving an exaggerated emphasis to any one aspect of the Jesus event, whether Jesus' birth, ministry, suffering, death, resurrection, or saving work. All of these "mysteries" of the Jesus event are disclosures of the divine mystery of selfless love as it explodes in Jesus. Focusing on love helps us grasp the connection and importance of each of these mysteries, without reducing each to the same intensity of the experience of love.

In the light of what I have just suggested, it seems entirely appropriate that our tradition has tended to emphasize the mystery of Jesus' death, at times singling it out as the saving event *par excellence*. In the light of our dark night of love, this seems entirely appropriate. As von Balthasar had already suggested, the dark night could make a fresh contribution in the area of "passiology." And so, in tune with this insight, von Balthasar views the passion and death as "the highest revelation of the trinity." For here we have the most selfless moment of love: "At this moment, the Word cannot hear itself. It collapses into its scream for the lost God," says von Balthasar rather daringly. Similarly, and perhaps under von Balthasar's influence, the International Theological Commission comments about Jesus' death: "The Fathers called this total mercy toward human pain and suffering 'the passion of love,' a love which in the passion of Jesus Christ has vanquished these sufferings and made them perfect." And let me mention Karl Rahner too, who argues that "the moment of . . . mystical union with God and the climax of . . . experience of the Spirit is present, in the last

resort"—in the death experience understood as a participation in the "chalice of Christ," in which one has "slowly
learned up to a point to taste fullness in the void, dawn in
doom, discovery in renunciation."[22]

Perhaps most importantly, a christology and soteriology
nourished by the dark night of selfless love helps us appreciate the specifically Jesus-like (or Christian) nature of the
disclosure of Divinity that meets us in the Jesus event. A
God which is Selfless Love is precisely the kind of Divinity
which does not hoard, but reaches out and overflows itself
into humanity. It is also the kind of God that does not destroy
humanity in the process: love does not violate the human
but creates and ennobles it. This would be a fruitful starting
point for a rethinking of the hypostatic union as a mystery
of divinity in humanity: selfless love drawing a radically free
human response. This would also be a fruitful place for a
thinking through of the uniqueness of Jesus, for the mystery
of the interchange of love admits of unique intensities of
response. But ultimately we come to the Divine Ground disclosed in the Jesus event, and it is here that a christology
formed through the dark night leads to radical insights. Martin Luther is a helpful example of a theologian and reformer
who did his God-thinking from the cross: recall his Heidelberg thesis 20:

> But he is rightly called a theologian who under-
> stands that part of God's being which is visible
> and directed towards the world to be presented
> in suffering and in the cross . . . true theology
> and true knowledge of God lie in Christ the cru-
> cified one.

Like Luther, I am suggesting that we probe the Jesus event
for what it reveals about God. A christology on the basis of
the dark night of selfless love would indicate that God reveals

Divinity as a Mystery of Selfless Love in the Jesus event. Curiously, too, Luther, in a commentary on Tauler's teaching about the mystical dark night, saw the eradication of the ego-filled self as the basic revelation coming from the cross:

> Although we might know that God does not work in us without first destroying us and what is our own (i.e. through a cross and suffering), still we are so foolish as to desire that the sufferings we undergo are only those which we choose or which we have read about or seen in the lives of others. Thus, we dictate to God the extent and form [of these sufferings], and are prepared to teach Him what He may do and how far He may go when he deals with us. We do not stand in sheer faith (*in mera fide*). . . . No . . . He disperses our plan (*consilium*) with a work that is the very reverse of it (*contrario opere*). . . . Thus, as [Tauler] says here, the whole of salvation is resignation of will in all things, whether spiritual or temporal—and naked faith (*nuda fides*) in God.

I have referred to Luther, because he draws a direct relationship between the mystical dark night and the cross. He is commenting upon Tauler's discussion of the birth of God in the soul of the mystic:

> In Job 17:12 we read, "*post tenebras spero lucem*," after the darkness we hope for the light. Hold yourself together! . . . Bear your suffering to the end and seek nothing else! . . . For, truly, when you stand this storm, the birth of God is close at hand, and God will be born in you. Take me at my word, when I say that no such anguish

arises in man except as God wants to bring forth
a new birth in him.

As the mystic dark night empties the self, so this kind of
emptiness is what is revealed to us at the cross. God comes
through in Jesus as radically empty. Luther saw that quite
explicitly, and it appears that his own background in medieval mysticism was a decisive aid in this.[23] St. Thérèse seems
to have learned this in her great dark night, too, when she
suggests that her night was a lesson in not measuring "the
divine power according to [one's] own narrow [mind]." Here,
I suggest, we link up with the theological and mystical tradition of kenoticism and abasement, reaching perhaps its
consummate expression in Pierre de Bérulle's "christology of
servitude" which has been seen as one of the basic sources
behind Thérèse. Listen to his "vow of servitude":

> O grand et admirable Jésus, je me rends à perpé-
> tuité votre esclave et de votre humanité adorable.
> En l'honneur de l'état et forme de serviteur que
> vous avez prise et à laquelle vous avez voulu ré-
> duire votre divinité en l'humanité, et votre hu-
> manité en l'état et la forme de vie qu'elle a me-
> née sur terre.[24]

I began this christological discussion by asking what
light the dark night experience might cast upon the mystery
of Jesus, and I suggested that it plays a corrective function,
pointing to the night or shadow side of this mystery. I would
suggest that that shadow side resides in the "broken," "ego-
less," "abased" and even "humiliated" form of love found in
the dark night. This is dark for most of us, and the mystics
would seem to indicate that it was likewise dark for Jesus
too. The fall into the dark abyss of emptiness seems to be
the kind of love we are speaking of in the Jesus event. Again,

I think this is a hard insight to see in a culture which takes its paradigms for love from the experience of romance primarily, and other forms of highly intimate love.

Let me add at this point the caution that perhaps Thérèse's great insights into christology might even need the corrective of the kind of collective dark night experience spoken of by Gustavo Gutierrez. For if we try to sympathetically think through christology from the experience of the dark night of the poor and oppressed, we come to an insight into the sociopolitical sting of the Jesus event as a mystery of love leading into an active struggle against the powers of violence in society. This is surely a quite ego-less kind of love, taking the dramatic form of martyrdom. Jürgen Moltmann is not precisely speaking of the dark night but of the medieval passion mysticism, but he gives expression to what I think Gutierrez has in mind by the collective dark night of his own people:

> This mysticism of the passion has discovered a
> truth about Christ which ought not to be sup-
> pressed by being understood in a superficial way.
> It can be summed up by saying that suffering is
> overcome by suffering, and wounds are healed by
> wounds.[25]

Surely a crucial dimension of the Jesus event is this sociopolitical dimension of Jesus' work on behalf of the poor and oppressed which led him to "overcome suffering through suffering, wounds through wounds." This is at least implicit in Thérèse's radically egoless love learned in her own dark night. But perhaps her own experience, limited more to the network of familial and convent relations, didn't enable her to surface this dimension of Jesus with the same amount of poignancy which we find in a Moltmann and a Gutierrez.

The ancient Church has traditionally traced the origin

of the Church to Jesus' own "dark night" of the passion and cross. Von Balthasar has written some beautiful lines on this theme:

> That the cross is solidarity, the ancient church
> has always seen in the figure of the cross itself:
> stretching out to all dimensions of the world,
> stretched out arms that want to embrace every-
> thing. The cross is, according to the *Didache, se-*
> *meion epektaseos* (sign of stretching out), and
> only God can achieve so wide a stretching: "God
> has stretched out his hands on the cross in order
> to encompass the limits of the earth" (Cyril of Je-
> rusalem); "God so stetched out his arms in his
> passion and embraced the earth in order to pre-
> signify that from the rising of the sun to its set-
> ting a future people would be gathered under his
> wings" (Lactantius). . . .[26]

This suggests the possible theological fruitfulness of our dark night experience for the theme of ecclesiology. For surely the Church, too, just like our anthropology and our chris-tology, needs to undergo the purification of the mystical dark night. Its corrective role for ecclesiology will be to insure that the Church, in its mission, ministry, and ritual, will be truly "stretched out" in that other-centered love seemingly only learned in the dark night. To my mind, Harvey D. Egan deserves special credit for pointing out the richness of the mystical experience as a source for our ecclesiological thought, and especially for indicating the connection be-tween our theme of the dark night and the theology of the Church. In his study of St. John of the Cross he notes that in *The Dark Night* John says that the mystic took "no other light or guide than the one that burned in my heart." And yet at the same time "he insisted that 'we must be guided humanly and visibly in all by the law of Christ the man and that of His Church and of His ministers' " in *The Ascent of Mount Carmel*. Harvey Egan interprets this tension between the purity of mystical experience and the need to participate in ecclesial life in this way: ". . . the night of faith through which mystics pass purifies and transforms their appreciation for and participation in scripture and Church." The dark night experience does not de-ecclesialize the mystic, but deepens and purifies one's ecclesial life. As Egan powerfully says, "In fact, both scripture and Church are demythologized, purified, healed, and transformed along with the mystic."[27]

As Egan points out the great connection between the dark night experience and our experience of the Church and our ecclesiology, let us pursue this line of thinking a bit more in our own context. How might the dark night experience, if truly attended to by the ecclesiologist, modify the great ecclesial triad of the Church's mission, ministry, and ritual?[28] The dark night critiques, perhaps, the tendency of the Church to think more of itself, its own institutions and ministers, its own laws and procedures, than of others. It calls the Church's mission back to the purifying trial of the dark night of being stretched out for others, like Jesus in his own dark agony. If you will, it forces ecclesiologists to attend to the shadow side and night side of the way the Church and theologians conceive of ecclesial mission. It seems to create ecclesiological turbulence.

In this respect, the images that come to mind are the typical post-Tridentine definition of the Church as the "perfect society" (*societas perfecta*) and the humble image of the Church as a servant stretched out in the dark night of selflessness for others. A Church that thinks of itself as "*perfecta*" has moved beyond attending to the dark night of purification. Most mystics that I am aware of don't draw an explicit connection between their own dark night experience and their thinking about the Church. They simply become reformers of the Church, trying to renew it in a way that helps it to be a bit more in accord with the stretched out Jesus of the Gospels. What makes Thérèse of Lisieux so re- markable is that she does explicitly connect our two themes, and that at a time when the *perfecta societas* image was certainly "in possession" among Roman Catholic theologians. We recall all the marvelous insights into theology and chris- tology coming from her remarkable night of faith. So, too, as she was experiencing her "Divine Furnace" and learning the "science of Love," she "understood that the Church had a Heart and that this Heart was burning with love. . . ."[29] But again, this is love as understood and purified by the dark night: not romanticized eros, but selfless *agape*, particularly of those we think to be especially "unlovable."

This rooting of ecclesial mission in the dark night of being stretched out in love leads to a notion of mission as continually open to critique. And so I would suggest that a thinking through of ecclesial mission in the light of the dark night leads to the need to consider sources which are likely to purify and stretch the Church. What might some of these be? History teaches us that at times the purification comes from the office-holders, from those in the rather more elite power positions. As people popularly but perhaps unhappily put it, "from the top." In recent times we might think of the courage of Pope John XXIII in calling the Second Vatican Council, of Pope Paul VI in seeing that council's reforms through as best he could. Or we might think of Anglican Archbishop Desmond Tutu and his struggle against South African apartheid, or of the Roman Catholic American bish- ops' peace pastoral, or the courageous statements of other episcopal conferences: one thinks of Medellín and Puebla, or of the Canadian bishops, for example. In these cases it is as if the ecclesial office-holders have gone through their dark night of purification on behalf of the Church, and now they are calling others to the same dark night passage. Their dark night is, if you will, the Church's own dark night *in miniature*.[30]

But there are other sources of ecclesial purification, as history teaches us. And an ecclesiology nourished on the dark night summons us to attend to them too. For example, at times groups of people within the greater Church, themselves having undergone the dark night passage in a particular way, maintain a dialectical, somewhat tension-filled, uneasy relationship with the larger Church organization. This *ecclesiola-in-ecclesia* (little Church within the greater Church) then acts as a kind of "outraged conscience"[31] for the greater Church, summoning it to purification. Is this not what the great Protestant Reformers had in mind? Is this not precisely the charism behind the great religious orders and congregations of Roman Catholicism, and behind the monastic renewal movements of all the churches? Let Saint Francis of Assisi, whose stigmata surely imply that he knew what the dark night was, stand as the representative example of what I have in mind. His "friars minor" or "lesser brothers" was an image of the kind of fraternity and renewal to which the Church was called, and he came to that vocation through the night: "Most high, glorious God, enlighten the darkness of my heart and give me, Lord . . . a perfect charity. . . ."[32] As his co-foundress, St. Clare, put it, ". . . for the Lord often reveals what is best to the lesser among us."[33]

Modesty requires, too, that we Church people remain open to the purification that can come from outside the "walls" of the Church. The dark night of purifying love transcends ecclesial barriers, as experience teaches, and as a universally loving God would seem to indicate. The somewhat "non-churched" can purify the Church, and have. I am thinking of the great movements for democratic reform in the western world. All too often these movements had to drag the greater churches to relinquish their role of legitimator of the political status quo. The dark night of struggle for the democratization of human rights came to the churches to some extent as a gift from beyond its frontiers. Think too of the struggle for the abolition of slavery at the civil war period. All too often the greater Church was the follower, not the leader. It was the purifying dark night of the black slaves, and then slowly of those who let themselves pass through that night in solidarity with the slaves, culminating in Abraham Lincoln's passion, that finally brought the churches to renewal. And then only in a fragmentary way. Perhaps, too, the dark night of the poor in South America is now revitalizing the greater churches, which now quite commonly speak of Jesus' preferential option for the poor. Is the dark night of enslaved and abused women now another furnace awaiting the greater churches?[34]

Mission, ministry, and ritual are interconnected realities in the Church. A purification of one should lead to a purification of the others. There is no question that the churches must have their ministers or priests as well as other office-holders who govern, lead, and guide the community in varying ways, helping it to stay away from chaos and preserve an "order of love." But there would seem to be a great amount of clericalism and elitism which cries out for the purifying fires of the dark night. In the light of the dark night, perhaps it is time to shelve the unhelpful distinction between "clergy" and "laity," which experience and studies have shown to foster the clericalist mentality. Perhaps the dark night is teaching us that it is possible to be priest or minister and not to be cleric.[35] The ministry, in other words, can still do much to represent the stretched out and selfless love that lies at the heart of the Church's mission. Roman Catholics and Eastern Orthodox need to pay special attention to the long and dark night of women's oppression. Most of us have arrived at the consensus that the systematic exclusion of women from the ministry or priesthood represents the failure of male dominated churches to open themselves to the stretching out process of the dark night. And, of course, ritual needs to be modulated in accord with the fluctuations in mission and ministry. Ritual is one of the great means by which the community remains community, nourishing itself on the great deeds of its past and remaining open to the renewal movements in its midst. Perhaps the Church's ritual life needs the dark night too. A ritualism which systematically excludes the faithful from the most important aspects of worship is not simply differentiating between priests and faithful but oppressing the latter. A declericalized and depatriarchalized ritual may be a part of the summons of the Church's dark night in our time. But we must not let our ecclesiology remain too insular. The dark night of poverty also needs attention. Mission, ritual, and ministry must stretch themselves out to the poor and oppressed. In fact, that remains the one essential summons of the cross. A ministry which does not manifest a solidarity with the poor's struggles rather than a privileged, elitist, and materially pampered lifestyle, and a ritual which does not at times shake us out of our lethargy and societal amnesia—these can hardly be said to be in conformity with the Jesus event.[36]

This talk about the Church's need for reformation or purification brings home to us the fragmentary and unfinished nature of our human and Christian existence. This is, of course, one of the blessings bestowed upon us in the dark night. As the Canadian bishops put it in their 1977 pastoral message: "As disciples of Christ, we cannot accept the idea that a paradise, an Ideal City, can be fully created here on earth."[37] Let us dwell a bit more, then, upon the theme of eschatology in the light of our mystical dark night.

There is a link between the experience of darkness and the expectation of things to come (= eschatology). It is as if an aspect of the dark night experience is to agitate us, flood us with a sacred unrest, and make us long for the light of knowledge and truth. Jesus, for example, does not know the timing of the end: "As to the exact day or hour, no one knows it . . . nor even the Son . . ." (Mk 13:32). Like everyone else, he experiences the night of the apocalyptic drama: "During that period . . . the sun will be darkened . . . (Mk 13:24). And it is this darkness which agitates him and causes him to say: "Be constantly on the watch!" (Mk 13:33). "Now we see indistinctly," said Paul (1 Cor 13:12), and few had the sense of eschatological expectation which he possessed. Interestingly, the Greek phrase here translated "indistinctly" (*in aenigmata*) can be translated "darkly" or "in darkness." Mystics, too, and other saints have traditionally had a strong yearning for the afterlife, and the dark night experiences (or its equivalents) have often played a role in this. St. Teresa of Avila's dark night of hell, for example, inspired this eschatological sensitivity in her:

> I was desiring to flee people and withdraw completely from the world. My spirit was not at rest, yet the disquiet was not a disturbing but a delightful one. It was obvious that it was from God and that His Majesty had given the soul heat so as to digest other heavier foods than those it was eating.[38]

The soul purified by the dark night, says John of the Cross, "will be a soul of heaven, heavenly and more divine than human. . . ." God fires "it divinely with love's urgent longing for God alone."[39]

So it seems that a first blessing of a theology attentive to the dark night experience is to pay renewed attention to the eschatological motif. Perhaps this is why there is a certain revitalization of the theme of eschatology and apocalyptic coming out of liberation and political theology, particularly the theology of Johannes Metz. The dark night of oppression sensitizes one to "the catastrophic nature of time itself," says Metz.[40] In this sense, it awakens our aspiration for more and for The More, while at the same time fostering a healthy critical stance toward the miseries of the present. It does both: this-worldly critique and other-worldly hopefulness. Here the various modulations of the dark night stare out at us: dark night as symbol of God's transcendent love, explosively disclosed in Jesus and awaiting us to some extent in the afterlife of eternity; dark night as symbolization of this world's finitude and sinfulness. Perhaps liberationist theologies tend to stress the latter; the traditional mystics, the former. The explosive power of the dark night is to expose us to all these modulations at once.

On a further level, I would suggest that the dark night experience can contribute some specific, if modest, insights into our eschatological future too. The final future we Christians await is not just some empty abyss, but one packed with the "content" of a divine encounter itself. This is perhaps why that future can fill us with hope and simultaneously with the ability to discern the miseries of the present as if by comparison with a "heavenly" alternative. A failure to engage in eschatological speculation, like our mothers and fathers in the faith engaged in it, could cripple this simultaneous dyad of hope and critique. Of course, all that follows falls under Karl Rahner's caution that our eschatological beliefs are not "photographic previews" of our ultimate desti-

nies but imaginative forecasts drawn from significant clues
provided us in past and present revelatory experiences, especially the Jesus event. Surely the dark night experience
should make us modest in our eschatological beliefs, sensi-
tizing us to our seeing only darkly, as Paul put it. But here
I am suggesting that the mystical dark night is itself, in its
various modulations, one of the crucial clues from which we
might draw our "imaginative eschatological drafts."[41]

Mystics usually draw a connection betwen the dark
night and hell, but let me begin with heaven. Of course,
heaven symbolizes that consummation of union with God
and humanity, and even with nature, that is looked upon as
the ultimate goal of the Christian life. If heaven is the consummation, what connection could there possibly be between the dark night and the dazzling light of eternal beatitude? Has not Charles Wesley exactly hit it when he said
of heaven that "There thy face unclouded see"?[42] Still, the
tradition has maintained that even the bliss of heaven does
not remove the incomprehensibility of God. "How unsearch-
able his ways," exclaims Paul of God (Rom 11:33), and even
Charles Wesley seems to indicate that the unlimited reality
of God requires the unlimited "span" of eternity to do it
justice:

> The painful thirst, the fond desire,
>> Thy joyous presence shall remove!
> But my full soul shall still require
>> A whole eternity of love.[43]

Even in "heaven"there remains something "dark" about the
Divine, something unknowable and toward which our "full
soul" is to be stretched, apparently.

Might not the mystics' dark night, at least in one of its
modulations, offer us a partial analogy and clue to this

strange beatific light which yet remains somehow dark? Karl Rahner had suggested that in the beatific vision our experience of the Mystery will be positive, a loving perichoresis between knowing and loving, in which the Mystery is happily affirmed rather than simply seen as a limit upon our cognitional powers.[44] Reaching back much further than Rahner, Maximus Confessor, who spoke of God as the "Inexhaustible," affirmed the existence of a certain kind of "fear" even in the bliss of heaven. This would not be the fear which stems from awareness of possible punishment. This kind of fear "is coupled with love itself and constantly produces reverence in the soul, lest through the familiarity of love it become presumptuous of God."[45] If I am not mistaken, the dark night of purification is, at least in one of its aspects, a defamiliarizing experience, one that restores awe and reverence just when domestication is liable to set in. Classical texts are found in the works of John of the Cross, Dionysius, and Gregory of Nyssa especially. Might I suggest that Gregory of Nyssa's notion of *epektasis*, of constantly reaching beyond to the Mystery, is a particularly fine example of a defamiliarization process? In any case, if we keep all of this in mind, we might find it credible to hold that the dark night can make its modest contribution even to the theology of heaven.

Of course, as I indicated earlier, texts abound on the interrelation between the dark night experience and the theology of hell, and even purgatory. Here the pain and purification of the night becomes a foretaste and sign of the purgation and possible hell to come. Recall the text from Teresa of Avila above, where she speaks of being "put in hell" in her dark night, where "it is the soul itself that tears itself in pieces." So, too, as Teresa knew, the mystic can pre-experience the sufferings of purgatory in her own dark experiences of purification.[46] Here there is nothing particularly new: the mystical experience serves an illustrative function, offering us a kind of experiential correlate to our eschatological beliefs.

An area which might bring about a genuine development in our eschatological thinking is the christological modulation of the dark night experience, spoken of earlier. Recall Thérèse of Lisieux' discovery of God as radical Charity in the Jesus event. Her dark night helped her understand the radically kenotic and selfless love of God shining through Jesus. Like Jesus, this caused Thérèse to beg "pardon for her brothers."[47] This discovery of a God of radical Charity could be developed in such a way that it means that no one is ever excluded from the divine love. Even the so-called "damned" would then be loved, and one could rightly ask whether we should speak of the "damned" at all in this case. Here we would have a foundation for a possibly orthodox form of apocatastasis. So far as I know, Von Balthasar, himself influenced by the hell experiences of Adrienne von Speyr, is the only theologian to pursue this path. A God of kenotic love does not destroy the sinner's freedom, but encounters "the sinner turned away from him in the form of weakness of the crucified," says Von Balthasar. In a statement deserving of much pondering, he says: "Even what we call 'hell' is, although it is the place of desolation, always still a christological place."[48] In other words, a theology of hell modified by the dark night of Jesus' entry into hell—modified by the radically selfless love of God revealed in Jesus—could lead to some cautious reformulations of our teaching on hell. In fact, all of our eschatological teaching, not just that of hell, needs to bring out its properly christological dimension if it is to be truly Christian. Perhaps this understanding of God as kenotic and the experience of this, experienced intensively in the mystical dark night, is that christological dimension.

Finally, I would suggest that an eschatology modified

by the kind of dark night experience spoken of by Gutierrez could go a long way in revitalizing the collective dimension of the afterlife. In this way, the tendency to privatize eschatology, by focusing only upon "my" personal end, might be corrected. The dark struggle of whole peoples to be freed from oppression is then a partial correlate to the coming of the kingdom and its painful "judgment" of the oppressor. Here is where we might place the dark night of oppressed women too. Might I suggest, too, that as we try to think through the collective dimensions of eschatology we try to avoid the kind of sick eschatology that paints the Divine in vindictive hues, a God who gives in to our urge for revenge? Attentiveness to the christological dimension of the dark night might be especially important in this regard.

Hopefully all of this is enough to make the case for the theological suggestiveness of the dark night. Perhaps it is now a little clearer why both speculative and practical forms of theology might want to consult the mystics on this rich theme. Of course there are other facets still, which we haven't mentioned at all. For example, theologians pursuing the dialogue with the non-Christian religions might find our theme rich in its possibilities. The "emptiness" to which the dark night leads is both a powerful participation in the Jesus-like God of Christianity and a possible route toward the rich "theology of emptiness" especially characteristic of some forms of Hinduism and Buddhism. Attentiveness to this theme could open us to these Eastern traditions, which in many respects have pursued this theme in a far more sustained way than have we in the West.[49]

Moral theologians might have something quite helpful to gain from a more sustained "ethical meditation" upon the dark night tradition. Philip S. Keane, in his superb study of the role of imagination in ethics, has suggested to me one possible link between our theme and ethical issues. Keane is trying to revitalize the need for non-conceptual and non-discursive approaches to ethics as a corrective to preponderantly conceptual and syllogistic approaches to moral decision-making. Hence his stress upon imagination as the creative womb and matrix from which good decision-making comes. In this respect he shows high regard for mysticism and the spiritual tradition in general as one of the guardians of the non-discursive dimension of reality. It is precisely here that I would see the moral dimension of the mystical dark night. For is not the dark night in one of its aspects a breaking down of our moral habits and ways of thinking, a kind of loosening up process, which opens us to new and perhaps challenging ways of thinking and acting? The dark night does not lead us to deny valid moral principles, but perhaps it might lead us to understand their limits, to apply them more accurately and "disinterestedly," and to be open to new applications of those same principles. For example, is the dark night of the threat of a nuclear holocaust an experience which has led the American Catholic bishops to a quite new application (not denial) of the principles of the natural law: given that threat, no nuclear war can be justified. I am sure that moralists will be able to think of other possibilities. The point is that we allow the dark night to teach us something about our moral theology.[50]

In bringing this excessively long study to a close, I find that I must "assault" the reader with at least two more issues. One is that of our own personal confirmation of what we have said through exploring correlates within our own experiences to the various modulations of this extremely dense dark night. For this study will remain terribly abstract and unconvincing if it does not stir us to see and/or to activate experiences which at least to some extent correspond to those of the mystics. Have we experienced the Divine as an "ever greater Horizon" for which we long? Have we come up against our mortal finitude and the more painful reality of our own narcissism? Have we been somehow "crushed" by the collective miseries of whole groups of peoples yearning and struggling for freedom from the dark night of bondage? And yet have we experienced a power which rocks us out of our egocentricity and "stretches" us out on the path of a quite selfless love? It would seem to me that these are the various modulations of the dark night as it finds expression in the shape of our existence.

Secondly, let us let the final word go, not to the night, but to the dawn. What keeps our dark night experience from derailing into sheer pessimism and utterly hopeless tragedy is the fact that it is one side of a two-sided dialectic. It is the night side of the day side of the Divine Mystery exploding into human experience. For this reason, the dark night itself needs a critique. If you will, a sign of the Christian authenticity of the dark night is its willingness to undergo its own purification. Might I suggest, then, that the reader move to the kind of "light" mysticism characteristic of the hesychast tradition, and especially characteristic of St. Gregory Palamas? Here one will find, not a denial of the "darkness," but a stress upon its light and dazzling side: ". . . it is in this dazzling darkness that the divine things are given to the saints." "Dazzling darkness" seems a marvelous phrase. It helps Gregory keep in focus the night as well as the dawn. For this reason he can say that "God is not only beyond knowledge" (= the darkness) but God is "also beyond unknowing (= the dazzling).[51] This is a good place to end.

Notes

[1]See chapter I.
[2]Ricoeur, "Biblical Hermeneutics," *Semeia* 4 (1975), 82.

[3]See the comments on Ricoeur and Tracy in the previous chapter. This citation: Ricoeur, *Essays on Biblical Interpretation* (Philadelphia: Fortress, 1980), p. 91.

[4]Citations: Gregory of Nyssa, *The Life of Moses* II, 162–163 (New York: Paulist, 1978), pp. 94–95; Dionysius the Areopagite, *The Divine Names and The Mystical Theology, The Mystical Theology* 2 (London: SPCK, 1940), pp. 194–195; Egan, p. 223; Thomas Merton, *The Climate of Monastic Prayer* (Spencer, MA: Cistercian Publications, 1969), p. 132; Gustavo Gutierrez, *We Drink from Our Own Wells: The Spiritual Journey of a People* (Maryknoll, N.Y.: Orbis, 1984), p. 129, and cf. pp. 83–88.

I find Ricoeur, *Essays on Biblical Interpretation*, pp. 100–101, very suggestive for the kind of literary comments made in my text. Basic historical overviews on the dark night theme: Rowan Williams, "Dark Night, Darkness," in Gordon S. Wakefield, ed., *The Westminster Dictionary of Christian Spirituality* (Philadelphia: Westminster, 1983), pp. 103–105; Michel Dupuy, "Nuit (Ténèbre)," in M. Viller *et al.*, eds., *Dictionnaire de Spiritualité*, XI (Paris: Beauchesne, 1982), cols. 519–525; Alain Gouhier, "Néant," *ibid.*, cols. 64–80; and Kenneth Leech, *Experiencing God: Theology as Spirituality* (New York: Harper & Row, 1985), pp. 162–198; Constance FitzGerald, "Impasse and Dark Night," in Joann Wolski Conn, *Women's Spirituality*, pp. 287–311.

[5]Ricoeur, *ibid.*, pp. 88–95; cf. his "The Power of Speech: Science and Poetry," *Philosophy Today* 29 (1985), 59–70.

[6]St. Teresa of Avila, "Cuán triste es, Dios mío," in *Complete Works of St. Teresa*, III, E. Allison Peers, ed. (London: Sheed and Ward, 1946), p. 285.

[7]St. John of the Cross, *The Dark Night* (*The Collected Works of St. John of the Cross*, p. 711).

[8]*Ibid.*, p. 712, and *The Living Flame of Love* (*ibid.*, p. 718).

[9]Baruzi, p. 196. Cf. Egan, pp. 171–173, and Georges Morel, *Le Sens de L'existence selon S. Jean de la Croix*, 3 vols. (Paris: Aubier, 1960–61), for a sensitivity to John's literary depth.

[10]St. Teresa of Avila, *The Book of Her Life* 32, 1–2 (*The Collected Works*, I, pp. 213–214).

[11]St. Thérèse of Lisieux, *Story of a Soul*, p. 211.

[12]See, most succinctly, Tracy, *The Analogical Imagination*, pp.

275–281, and Ricoeur, "The Narrative Function," in John B. Thompson, ed., *Paul Ricoeur: Hermeneutics and the Human Sciences*, pp. 274–296; Ricoeur's magisterial work on the theme is *Time and Narrative*, 2 vols. (Chicago: University of Chicago, 1984–85).

[13]*Pastoral Constitution on the Church in the Modern World* 13, *The Documents of Vatican II*, Walter M. Abbott, ed. (New York: America Press, 1966), p. 212.

[14]Karl Rahner is especially good on the theme of God as Horizon of Mystery; cf., for example, "The Experience of God Today," *Theological Investigations* XI (New York: Seabury, 1974), pp. 149–165.

[15]Gregory of Nyssa, *The Life of Moses* II, 239, p. 116. For an example of rationalistic theologies, see Gerald A. McCool, *Catholic Theology in the Nineteenth Century: The Quest for a Unitary Method* (New York: Seabury, 1977), esp. pp. 17–36 and James C. Livingston, *Modern Christian Thought: From the Enlightenment to Vatican II* (New York: Macmillan, 1971), *passim*. The most sensitive but succinct treatment of atheism I have seen is John Macquarrie, *In Search of Deity: An Essay in Dialectical Theism* (New York: Crossroad, 1985), esp. pp. 43–56.

[16]*The Cloud of Unknowing* 44, William Johnston, ed. (Garden City, New York: Doubleday & Co., 1973), p. 103, and St. John of the Cross, *The Dark Night* I, 12, 2 (*The Collected Works*, p. 321).

[17]Gutierrez, p. 11.

[18]Galilea, p. 52.

[19]*The Cloud of Unknowing* 44, p. 104.

[20]St. Thérèse of Lisieux, *Story of a Soul*, pp. 205–229 at 205, 209–216, 218–219. She often speaks of the "expansion" of the heart or self (cf., for example, p. 237). Gouhier, cols. 73–79, is helpful on St. Thérèse.

[21]*Theology, Christology, Anthropology* (Washington, D.C.: USCC, 1983), pp. 10–11. This document seems highly influenced by Hans Urs von Balthasar, himself greatly influenced by Thérèse, as we have seen.

[22]*The Von Balthasar Reader*, pp. 148–149; *ibid.*, p. 20; and Karl Rahner, "Experience of the Holy Spirit," pp. 206–207.

[23]Luther, Heidelberg thesis 20, as cited in Moltmann, *The*

Crucified God, p. 211, from Martin Luther, *Werke: Kritische Ges-amtausgabe* (Weimar: Herman Böhlau und Nachfolger, 1883ff), I, p. 355; and Steven E. Ozment, *Homo Spiritualis: A Comparative Study of the Anthropology of Johannes Tauler, Jean Gerson and Martin Luther (1509–16) in the Context of Their Theological Thought* (Leiden: E. J. Brill, 1969), pp. 200–201, translating from Luther's *Werke* IX, pp. 102.10ff, and from Tauler's *Die Predigten Taulers*, Ferdinand Vetter, ed. (Berlin, 1910), pp. 172.7ff.

[24]As cited in Fernando Guillèn Preckler, *"Etat" chez le Cardinal de Bérulle: Théologie et spiritualité des "etats" bérulliens* (Rome: Gregorian University, 1974), pp. 106–107, from Marseille folios 61–65 ("O great and admirable Jesus, in perpetuity I pledge myself the slave even of your adorable humanity. I do this in honor of the state and form of servant which you have assumed and to which you have wished to reduce your divinity in humanity, and your humanity in the state and form of life to which you have been led while on earth" [My translation]); Gouhier, col. 73, has noted the connection between the theology of Kenosis in Bérulle and Thérèse. Guillèn Preckler sees the continuation of this Berullian theme of servitude in a theology of service on behalf of others, and especially points to Von Balthasar's theology of kenosis as one such example in *Bérulle Aujourd'hui: Pour une spiritualité de l'humanité du Christ* (Paris: Beauchesne, 1978), pp. 64–65n39.

[25]Moltmann, *The Crucified God*, p. 46.

[26]*The Von Balthasar Reader*, p. 215.

[27]Egan, pp. 170–171.

[28]See Rosemary Radford Ruether, *Sexism and God-Talk: Toward a Feminist Theology* (Boston: Beacon, 1983), pp. 193–213, for this ecclesiological triad.

[29]St. Thérèse of Lisieux, *Story of a Soul*, pp. 188, 187, 194. A good overview of the *perfecta societas* model of the Church can be found in Avery Dulles, *Models of the Church* (Garden City, New York: Doubleday & Co., 1974), pp. 31–42. Dulles cites as an example the view of the Church from the proposed schema of Vatican I on the Church: "We teach and declare: The Church has all the marks of a true society. Christ did not leave this society undefined and without a set form. Rather, he himself gave its existence, and his will determined the form of its existence and gave

it its constitution. The Church is not part nor member of any other society and is not mingled in any way with any other society. It is so perfect in itself that it is distinct from all human societies and stands far above them" (pp. 33–34, from J. Neuner and H. Ross, *The Teaching of the Catholic Church* [Staten Island, N.Y.: Alba House, 1967] No. 361, pp. 213–214). Placing Thérèse's definition of the Church next to Vatican I's brings out something of her daring originality, as Joann Wolski Conn has indicated to us before (in chapter I).

[30]Woods, pp. 165–166, is quite helpful on this notion.

[31]*Ibid.*, p. 169, for this phrase. Karl Rahner, *The Dynamic Element in the Church*, pp. 42–83, is quite helpful on this notion of tension between the *ecclesiola* and the *ecclesia*.

[32]*Francis and Clare: The Complete Works* (New York: Paulist, 1982), p. 103 (from Francis' prayer before a crucifix).

[33]*Ibid.*, p. 216 (from Clare's *Rule*).

[34]See Gutierrez and FitzGerald for a sensitivity to South America's and women's dark night. For the black issue, see the suggestive works of Elton Trueblood, *Abraham Lincoln: Theologian of American Anguish* (New York: Harper and Row, 1973), and Peter C. Hodgson, *New Birth of Freedom: A Theology of Bondage and Liberation* (Philadelphia: Fortress, 1976), esp. pp. 2–41.

[35]On issues dealing with ministry, I recommend Thomas Franklin O'Meara, *Theology of Ministry* (New York: Paulist, 1983). For the "clergy-laity" distinctions, see his pp. 161–167.

[36]On the place of ritual, I recommend, besides Wainwright's great work, the helpful study of George S. Worgul, Jr., "Ritual as the Interpreter of Tradition," *Louvain Studies* X (1984), 141–150.

[37]From "A Society To Be Transformed," Pastoral Message of the Catholic Bishops of Canada, Dec. 1, 1977, as found in Gregory Baum and Duncan Cameron, *Ethics and Economics: Canada's Catholic Bishops on the Economic Crisis* (Toronto: James Lorimer & Co., 1984), Appendix 3, pp. 170–179 at 176.

[38]St. Teresa of Avila, *The Book of Her Life* 32, 8 (*The Collected Works* I, p. 216).

[39]St. John of the Cross, *The Dark Night* 2, 13, 11 (*The Collected Works*, p. 361).

[40]Johann Baptist Metz, *Faith in History & Society*, p. 176.

[41]Cf. Rahner, "The Hermeneutics of Eschatological Assertions."

[42]From Hymn 112.10, as cited in *John and Charles Wesley: Selected Writings and Hymns* (New York: Paulist, 1981), p. 287.

[43]Hymn 51.9 in *ibid.*, p. 230.

[44]"The beatific vision does not of course annul God's incomprehensibility (*D* 428; 1782). It is rather the direct experience and loving affirmation of God as incomprehensible. His mystery is not merely the limit of finite cognition, but its ultimate positive ground and final goal, the beatitude of which consists in the ecstatic raising and merging of cognition, without suppressing it, into the bliss of love. In God, as the origin and goal of all reality that is not God, all other reality is known and loved, in the manner and measure in which it concerns us (cf. Aquinas, *Summa Theologica*, III, q. 10, a. 2)," says Karl Rahner in "Beatific Vision," *Sacramentum Mundi* I (New York: Herder and Herder, 1968), pp. 151–153 at 153.

[45]St. Maximus Confessor, *The Four Hundred Chapters on Love* 3, 46 and 1, 81, in *Maximus Confessor: Selected Writings* (New York: Paulist, 1985), pp. 67 and 44.

[46]St. Teresa of Avila, *The Book of Her Life* 38, 29 and 31 (*The Collected Works*, I, pp. 266–267). Cf. also the important experience of and teaching upon purgatory in *St. Catherine of Genoa: Purgation and Purgatory, The Spiritual Dialogue* (New York: Paulist, 1979).

[47]St. Thérèse of Lisieux, *Story of a Soul*, p. 212.

[48]*The Von Balthasar Reader*, p. 422.

[49]See, for example, Keiji Nishitani, *Religion and Nothingness* (Berkeley: University of California, 1982). This subject of the link between Christian *kenosis* and Buddhist emptiness has been studied by Hans Waldenfels, *Absolute Nothingness: Foundations for a Buddhist-Christian Dialogue* (New York: Paulist, 1980).

[50]Keane, *Christian Ethics and Imagination*, pp. 41–44; on pp. 9–11 he speaks of imagination's ability to help us apply moral principles in new and creative ways and in this context describes how life's crises (our dark night?) might birth such imaginative applications of principles: "At certain stages in our moral development,

carefully worked out applications may well be all we can handle. But in the challenging crises of life, people will often have to move toward new and not so standard applications, applications which do not deny our principles but rather apply them in new ways to new cases. Many persons' moral development will not be able to proceed adequately if they cannot learn to move beyond the cautious applications to more creative ones" (p. 11).

[51]St. Gregory Palamas, *The Triads* I.111.18 and I.111.4 (pp. 36 and 32).

VII

St. John of the Cross as Pneumopathologist: A Mystic's Hermeneutics of Suspicion

Today there seems to be a renewal of interest in, almost a "rehabilitation" of, the category of moral evil or sin in western theology. To a great extent this seems to be related to cultural phenomena, which in turn produce their theological modulations. The optimism and world affirmation somewhat characteristic of western nations from the Renaissance and early Enlightenment on have had to be modified by the horrors of the French Revolution's bloody reign of terror, by two world wars, by the Nazi holocaust and the Soviet Gulags, by Vietnam with its loss of U.S. American "innocence," by the atrocities in modern Asia and Africa, by the ecological "crisis," and now the ultimate catastrophe of a possible nuclear holocaust of the globe. Thus the more optimistic thinkers of the "early" Enlightenment—like Hume, Locke, and Kant—have had to be modified by the more sanguine "archaeologists" of the irrational in human beings and society who make up the "late" or "second" Enlightenment—namely, Nietzsche, Freud, Jung, Marx, Durkheim, Weber, etc. Humans, so we have been forced to remember once again, are not simply "ruled" by the rational and meaningful. Somehow they become twisted and mean, lashing out in the most irrational ways, and even in ways that seem "ungraspable" or unconscious to themselves.

In contemporary theology, political and liberation theologians seem particularly sensitive to this sinfully dark side of humanity, and they have sought to learn anew how to suspect and expose evil wherever it may be found, often through some kind of "dialogue" with the modern masters of suspicion mentioned above and attunement to the Christian tradition. Feminist theologians, too, have listened to the voices of abused and oppressed women, and this has led them to a creative feminist rethinking of our Christian heritage. And this feminist rethinking goes along with a powerful exposé of the pathology of misogynism. Practical theologians, in other words, deserve a great deal of credit for a renewed sense of the suspicion of evil and sin in our contemporary theology. And this is having its repercussions in other areas of theological thought. Christologians are more attuned to the link between christology and soteriology, striving to surface how totally concerned with the problem of human iniquity and the attempt to be liberated from that the Jesus event really is. Our theology of God even requires rethinking in the light of the mystery of sin and moral evil: How can God be credible in the light of the holocaust and Gulag? The list could go on. The pathological dimension of human existence seems ubiquitous. Once it is exposed it seems to force us theologians to rethink everything at least partially in its light.

In this chapter I would like to recommend John of the Cross to the person seeking to refine her or his capacities to suspect and expose human evil and sin. "Pneumopathology," the study of the sinfully dark side of humanity, is surely something which reaches a kind of systematic and sustained development in the works of John. I have in mind especially his *The Ascent of Mount Carmel* and *The Dark Night*, although these need to be balanced by the other writings. John, of course, is not wholly original. His work forms a part of a great tradition. For both Judaism and Christianity are soteriological religions: they are concerned with being saved or "liberated" from evil and sin. Thus, there is a long and quite sophisticated tradition within these religions of grappling with and reflecting upon the mystery of human iniquity. Surely the prophets knew a great deal about human malice, even on the societal level. Think of the searing critiques of Amos and Hosea. "Ephraim has surrounded me with lies, the house of Israel, with deceit," said Hosea (12:1), who, like the other prophets, was something of a master at exposing the iniquitous underside of people and nation. Think, too, of the biblical notion of the "hardening of heart," which at least on one of its levels I take to be an awareness of our ability to create a "false consciousness,"[1] to hide ourselves from the depths of our own depravity. Here we have a close biblical parallel to the notion of the deep kind of evil and sin, the kind which remains "unconscious" and "masked." "Harden not your hearts as at Meribah, as in the day of Massah in the desert," proclaims Psalm 95:8 representatively of this rich biblical tradition of "suspicion" (cf. Ex 8:32; 9:34–35; Dt 15:7; 1 Sam 6:6; 2 Chr 36:13; Heb 3:8, 15; 4:7, etc.).[2] Think, too, of Jesus' ability to unmask sin's many manifestations as well as its final source:

> What emerges from within a man, that and nothing else is what makes him impure. Wicked designs come from the deep recesses of the heart; acts of fornication, theft, murder, adulterous conduct, greed, maliciousness, deceit, sensuality, envy, blasphemy, arrogance, an obtuse spirit. All these evils come from within and render a man impure (Mk 7:20–23).

Jesus' remarkable ability to expose evil and trace it to its funding source in the perverted heart represents a kind of brilliant continuation of the hardening of the heart tradition, and later Christian thinkers have taken it up and given it their own helpful twist. Think of Paul's grappling with this in Romans: "My inner self agrees with the law of God, but I see in my body's members another law at war with the law of my mind" (7:22–23; cf. 7:13–25; Gal 5:16–26). Think, too, of St. Augustine's brilliant analysis of human bondage and perversity, in his own *Confessions* and again in *The City of God,* especially Books 13 and 14. ". . . it was not the corruptible flesh that made the soul sinful; it was the sinful soul that made the flesh corruptible," he says.[3] And one can trace a continuation and a development of this Christian tradition of reflecting upon human evil and sin down through the desert mothers and fathers, the monastic theologians, the moral tracts and theologians, and of course in the great mystics who struggled with the dark side of themselves and others as they tried to move toward greater union with God. John of the Cross needs to be seen against this horizon. The phenomenon that he is would be inconceivable apart from this larger tradition.[4]

And, of course, the study of human pathology is a phenomenon that even transcends the Jewish and Christian traditions. All forms of soteriology are concerned with it, and so we find enormously complex forms of speculation on our topic in the Hindu and Buddhist orbits, and indeed in most other religions. The Greek-Classic tradition of the west was also a form of soteriology, concerned with the restoration of order in soul and society. It was a kind of therapy, in other words, and it might be helpful to say something more about this, for it helps us see something more of the background of John of the Cross, which at least indirectly was influenced by the classical inheritance.[5]

I consider the remarkable work of Eric Voegelin to be of first importance in this entire area of the classical tradition's contribution to pneumopathology, and indeed in the

area of pneumopathology in general.⁶ Voegelin has shown
how the problem of "existential disorder" through the closure
of the soul to the "ground of reality" (a classical parallel to
the biblical hardening of the heart) was well known and reflected upon at least a century before Plato and Aristotle.
Heraclitus spoke of the men living in the illusionary private
worlds of their imaginations, the sleepwalkers mistaking their
illusions for reality. Aeschylus spoke of the disease of human
madness. And Plato combined the insights of both Heraclitus
and Aeschylus in the *Republic* when he spoke of the soul
whose disease blinds him to the way he brings about societal
disorder. But Voegelin thinks that pneumopathology reached
a special clarity among the Stoics, who were struggling with
"the shattering experiences of ecumenic imperialism and, in
its wake, existential disorientation as a mass phenomenon."⁷
The Stoics create the term "alienation" (*allotriosis*), and know
about a madness of the soul or what Cicero calls *morbi an-
imorum* ("diseases of the mind") in the *Tusculan Disputations*.⁸ They also struggle over the difference between symptoms and source. It is natural to dwell upon the symptoms
of soul sickness, such as the disordered use of the human
passions and body, and other mental states of anxiety, desire
for fame, etc. "But a symptomatology of this kind, though
valuable as an approach on the common sense level, is an-
alytically not precise enough," says Voegelin.⁹ For it is not
the passions or reason which are evil, but their misuse
through *agnoia*, the psyche closed to open searching. Here,
it seems to me, the classical tradition joins with the Christian. The former possibly even influenced the New Testament tradition, but there can be little doubt that John of the
Cross drinks from both wells, although quite originally.

   I hope the reader will take time out to read the *Ascent*
and the *Night*, the two major sources of "sanjuanist" pneumopathology. At least I would look at them at this point, and

then perhaps read or reread them after finishing this little essay. Also it will be well to begin with some literary considerations, keeping in mind the role of the literary form or genre, as we have indicated before. Especially is this important in the case of John, who is a quite self-consciously literary artist and master. To begin with the literary dimension is to follow the natural movement of interpretation, as we have previously indicated: from the sense encoded in the text to the possible references or worlds of meaning opened up in front of the text.

Both the *Ascent* and the *Night* are a combination of poetry and prose commentary, with the one poem, *The Dark Night,* governing both. As we have shown before, the "dark night" is a standard symbol with varied levels of depth. As a symbol or metaphor, it abolishes the ordinary sense world of reference in favor of a spiritual, transcendent world of meaning. And that world of meaning might be the transcendence of God, the finitude of man, or even the evil and sinful side of humans taken individually and collectively. The very symbolism of "dark night" is a kind of emphatic negation or "intensified" negation summoning forth the dark side of God (= divine transcendence) or the dark side (= finitude) or night side (= sin, both personally and collectively) of human beings. To enter into this symbol is to expose oneself to these levels of meaning.

But John incorporates the dark night symbolism into a poem, and this surely adds some new literary modulations to the symbol. For one thing, the dark night theme is somehow repeated in each of the eight stanzas, and this surely heightens the symbol's already intensified nature. If you will, the poem prolongs the intensive negation of the symbol. The poem, by the progression through the stanzas, is also able to disclose the varied depths of the symbol. Each stanza is not simply repetitive: there is an element of entry into varied depths as one moves through the poem. The poem also has about it a kind of lover's private dialogue quality, but appropriately the Beloved is spoken about rather than directly addressed: even this intimacy is somewhat "dark." But this aspect of the poem surfaces the fact that the darkness is the negative side of a more positive relationship with the Divine Beloved: it is not sheer pessimism. If you will, the poem is like a "chant" which one sings, and this again highlights the essentially positive nature of the whole process. Thus, from the viewpoint of our theme of pathology, the poem will move the reciter into varied levels of this reality, making one into a veritable "archaeologist" of human pathology. At the same time, the supporting relationship to the Beloved, as it breaks forth in the chanted poem, preserves this intensive exposure to pathology from derailing into simple negativity.[10]

There is also a relationship between poem and commentary, a kind of dialogue between them. Might this not express, in literary mode, the relationship between the entry into the dark night and ourselves? As the commentary engages in dialogue with the poem, so perhaps are we invited to enter into this movement. In a sense, the commentary is "us" as we move into the depths of the night. As Georges Morel has suggested, the passage from commentary to poem is like the passage from the dispersed or fragmented (can I say "broken"?) nature of our ordinary existence to the more profound, integrated, and unified existence of the mystic's existence. "The commentary expresses a project and the poem a result," says Morel. The dark night "is chanted in the poem, that is to say, it is taken up and transfigured in consequence of the action of God, and the commentary gives us a detailed recital of this, but the idea of this death must not be confused with the reality of the death," he adds.[11] It is the passage from beginner's idea to mystic's reality that the movement between commentary and poem helps us to experience. Now, what might some of our discoveries be, particularly into human pathology, as we enter into this movement?

There is a difference between being a "fool for Christ's sake" and simply a "plain, damned fool," said Reinhold Niebuhr, himself an important archaeologist of evil and sin.[12] The latter lives in an illusionary world, masking from self the night side of human existence. Now it seems to me that it is this tendency to live in illusion, to pretend that all is day and to ignore the night, it is this tendency which John of the Cross wants to shatter. ". . . we are not writing on pleasing and delightful themes addressed to the kind of spiritual people who like to approach God along sweet and satisfying paths," says John. On the contrary, given the harsh reality of our "inordinate appetites" and "imperfections," we must "ordinarily pass through" the night of purification on our journey toward union with God. "One dark night . . . My house being now all stilled . . ." says John in the poem's first stanza. That is, this night requires the "stilling" of the totality of our disordered urges and imperfections (= "house"). John is trying to create in us, with God's help, a critical consciousness and praxis. At this point John links up with the tradition of the critique of the dark, sinful side of human existence found in the biblical and classical traditions. But as we've indicated, his work actually initiates us into this critical tradition and intensifies our experience of it.[13]

A second sanjuanist contribution is the avoidance of both utopianism and pessimism. If history is any indication, it is not at all easy to avoid these two extreme errors when one is in the wilderness of evil and sin. The pain of evil either drives one to derail into utopian dream worlds, or so hardens one that any reserves of hopefulness are dried up. Yet St. John dwells in the in-between. He clearly avoids pessimism, for he thinks it is possible to achieve liberation: "In remaining unattached . . . a person is unencumbered and free to love all rationally and spiritually, which is the way God wants him to love," says John in his commentary. So, too, there is a positive celebration of liberation throughout the stanzas of the poem: "Ah, the sheer grace!" chants the first two stanzas. And this "grace" is prolonged throughout the poem: "O night more lovely than the dawn! . . . Transforming the beloved in her lover" (fifth stanza); "I went out from myself, Leaving my cares Forgotten among the lilies" (eighth stanza).[14]

But this hopefulness of grace, while intensive and even lyrical in the poem, remains critical of utopianism. In the commentary portion of the *Ascent*, perhaps Prologue 3 is the key text here, for John notes that many souls "do not advance" into the dark night for varied selfish reasons. Elsewhere John will indicate that God calls all to the full flowering of the mystical life. And so he is hopeful. But here in the *Ascent-Night* he concentrates on the arduousness of the path and on the few who seem to respond to the divine summons. In the poem itself John repeats "My house being now all stilled" twice (first and second stanzas), as if to bring home the difficulties involved. So, too, he only addresses these works to his fellow Carmelites, who have not only asked him for this work but "are already detached to a great extent. . . ." Perhaps most importantly, throughout poem and commentary, the night remains the night. John does not try to abolish human and divine reality. Humans will struggle, and as they do they will advance into varied depths of the night: from "evening" through "midnight" on to "early dawn just before the break of day." But the night persists, nonetheless. Most importantly, "God is also a dark night to man in this life," says John. God remains the ever greater one.[15]

A third feature of the sanjuanist pneumopathology is its totalistic character, at least in its main thrust. Herein lies, I think, one of John's crucial contributions to a contemporary hermeneutics of suspicion. For he seems to be aware that we humans, despite our great calling, can pervert almost anything, and in fact will have a tendency to do so. John is not selective or narrow in what he would be suspicious of, despite the pressures exercised by society and Church. This ability to suspect all, I suggest, lies behind the daring and rigorous negations (*nadas*) in Book I, 6 and 11 of the *Ascent:*

> Endeavor to be inclined always: . . .
> not to want something, but to want nothing; . . .
> and desire to enter into complete nudity, empti-
>   ness, and poverty
> in everything in the world.
> To reach satisfaction in all
> desire its possession in nothing. . . .
> To arrive at being all
> desire to be nothing.
> To come to the knowledge of all
> desire the knowledge of nothing. . . .
> And when you come to the possession of the all
> you must possess it without wanting anything.[16]

This is a quite radical kind of critique, I think, which in some sense seems to enable John to "transcend" both his own personal preferences-interests-inclinations, as well as those of his society and Church.

There are various ways in which John expresses this need to critique all throughout the *Ascent* and the *Night*. Here we seem to enter upon conflictual territory in sanjuanist studies, so what I offer now is only a proposal "stimulated" by a sensitivity to the hermeneutics of suspicion.[17] First, there are the "totalistic negations/*nadas*" throughout both works, which continually remind the reader that the aim is the critique of all—there are no privileged exceptions.

The repetition of the line from the poem's first stanza—"My house being now all stilled"—perhaps announces the theme the best. That is, I (or "my house") must negate all the inclinations of myself. What the poem expresses poetically is both reinforced by the great *nada* poem cited above as well as by the commentary. For example, the *Ascent* rigorously states that "all the goodness of creatures in the world compared with the infinite goodness of God can be called evil, since nothing is good, save God only." The aim is to be freed from all sources of corruption: "It makes little difference whether a bird is tied by a thin thread or by a cord."[18] It should be kept in mind that this radical negation is not a denigration of created reality: down that path lies gnosticism. John seems to be negating our disordered use of creation: "I am speaking of the voluntary appetites, because the natural ones are little or no hindrance at all," says John.[19] It seems to be our disordered use of the appetites, through which we can pervert anything—that is the object of John's rigorous *nada*. The *nada* is total, not because everything is evil, but because we can pervert anything, in other words.

A second way in which John gives expression to his totalistic critique is through the differentiation between the dark night of the senses and the dark night of the spirit. Here John is dependent upon the philosophy of human faculties characteristic of late Scholasticism, which distinguishes sense and spirit in the human being. The distinction should not be read as a separation; soul and body interpenetrate in scholastic theology. But John's presentation lends itself to thinking in terms of separation, since he rather too neatly divides his treatment of the two nights. Still, he can't have a complete separation in mind, for he traces the corruption of the sensory dimension of humans to the disordered psyche, as we shall see. The fact that he speaks of voluntary appetites illustrates the interpenetration between sense and spirit too. More important in our context is the totalistic nature of the sanjuanist critique. Body and spirit or sense and spirit give expression to the totality of the human person—it is the whole person which falls into perversion and so needs to undergo the purifying fires of the night. The two nights are a symbol for the totality of the human person as it falls into pathology and needs the purification of liberation. Perhaps today we might say that both our vision (spirit) and our praxis (senses) need to be liberated.

Here I might recommend that the reader "dwell" for a while upon the subtle manifestations of "sense" and "spirit" which John diagnoses. While it might at times seem somewhat artificial (a part of the negative legacy of scholastic faculty philosophy) to break the senses and spirit up into various parts, ignoring the holistic nature of humans, still the varied "parts" or elements can actually promote a sensitivity and attunement to the subtle dimensions of our sensory-spiritual totality. Having a sense for subtlety—for the rhythms, changes, and distinct manifestations of our human self—is not the same as lapsing into a kind of separatistic-dualistic faculty psychology-philosophy. John was very subtle, and he can guide us toward a similar subtlety. Thus there is a way in which we can critically appropriate John's analyses of the ways in which we can pollute our exterior sense faculties of seeing, hearing, smelling, tasting, or touching, as well as our inner sense faculties of fantasy and imagination—all of which constitute the sanjuanist sensory night. Or, to turn to the night of the spirit, of the ways in which we can pollute intellect, memory, and will.[20] We need a subtle sensitivity to the manifold possibilities of human perversion, physically (the senses), intellectually and unconsciously (the spirit), do we not? Thus, as John exclaims, "The variety of filth caused in the soul is both inexplicable and unintelligible. . . . It would be a surprise and a pity to observe how only one inordinate act can in its own way occasion innumerable kinds and various degrees of filth;"[21] we need to appropriate this imaginatively. Under his guidance we can learn to develop our own analysis of evil.

A third expression of John's totalistic symptomatology of evil is the confusing distinction between the "active" and the "passive" nights of purification. The reader may be aware that John treats the "active" night of the senses and spirit in the *Ascent*, while he reserves his treatment of the "passive" night of the same to the *Night*. This distinction between "active" and "passive" is difficult and confusing. John clearly does not mean that the active night is a completely human project with no element of God's aid in it, for he speaks of God being the one who introduces people to this night. Thus in some sense the active night also possesses its passive (God-initiated) dimension. But, still he tells us that in the "passive way an individual does nothing, for God accomplishes the work in him, while he acts as the recipient."[22] At first blush this sounds like the passive night has no human element in it, but note that he speaks of the person *acting* as a recipient. So there is some human action (an active dimension) even in the passive night. What, then, does John intend? Apparently we are dealing with a distinction used by the mystics (perhaps not entirely happily) to focus the mystics' experience that as they grow in purification they become a more finely tuned instrument or sacrament of the divine Presence: self and God so agree or compenetrate that one seems to experience God's presence in an overwhelming manner. If this be an acceptable interpretation, then the "active/passive" distinction is again a symbolism by which John wants to express the total nature of the transformation which the mystic must undergo. That is, the entire agent (the active dimension) must negate every obstacle to being a finely tuned expression of the Divine. As and when this occurs, we can speak of the passive night. This would be to become "God through participation," as John daringly puts it.[23] One feels that by singling out the "passive" element in this manner John intensifies the total nature of his critique: our *whole* humanity must become a divine expression.

Up to this point we have stressed the total nature of John's "archaeology" of evil in a rather more intensive, "spatial," and vertical manner: it is the whole person from bottom to top and top to botton in his or her psychosomatic unity which must undergo the fires of purification from narcissistic self-interest. The genius of John is his ability to expose us to the enormously complex modulations of our ability to be iniquitous. And so there is also a more extensive, "temporal," and horizontal approach to human pathology in the *Ascent-Night*. The poem itself, of course, expresses this temporality of the night: one must *move through* the poem, as one must *move through* the night. And one must *move* from commentary (announcing the project) to the poem (actualizing the project). In other words, there is a temporal movement involved. Freedom from egocentric self-interest is an historical project. Note the journey motif: "The journey . . . does not consist in recreations, experiences, and spiritual feelings, but in the living, sensory and spiritual, exterior and interior death of the cross."[24] Not only human verticality/ spatiality but even human horizontality/temporality comes under "suspicion" and "critique." Note, too, the sanjuanist use of the traditional "stages" of the spiritual life, from purgation, through illumination, and on toward union, which run through the *Ascent-Night*. Of course, these stages can be seen as interpenetrating dimensions of the night on one level, and John seems to do this. For example, the entire night is a purification with its illuminative and unitive aspects. Yet John reserves the language of illumination and union for the later stages of the mystical journey, and this promotes a more temporal orientation in his work. So, too, will John speak not only of *the* night, but of varied phases of the night. Evening (purgation), midnight (illumination), and dawn (beginnings of union) surely underscore the temporal dimension.

Despite this apparent attempt to be totalistic in critiquing evil and sin, is John not too privatistic in the *Ascent-Night?* After all, the dominating model seems to be that of the individual mystic as he or she undertakes the arduous journey of the night. Does this "privatism" not perhaps blind John to the evil and corruption of the Church and society within which he lives? Of course, we know that John was a reformer of his Church (and thus, indirectly, of his society) through his work with St. Teresa of Avila in reforming Carmel. But here we are asking whether John has reflectively articulated the need for ecclesial and social suspicion. I would suggest that it surfaces. The ecclesial critique is subdued but present in John's view that the practices of the Church (especially here the images of God and the saints, questioned by the Lutheran Reformers) can be "the cause of many delusions and dangers." These, too, require the *nada:* "Images will always help a person toward union with God, provided that he does not pay more attention to them than is necessary, and that he allows himself to soar . . . from the painted image to the living God. . . ."[25]

And I suggest that John extends his suspicion of evil to society as a whole too. This "inchoate" social critique finds expression, for example, in the use of the Johannine image of the battle between light and darkness (John cites Jn 1:15). In the same context he will employ the Pauline image of the world and its foolishness (cf. 1 Cor 3:18–19). "All the sovereignty and freedom of the world compared with the freedom and sovereignty of the Spirit of God is utter slavery, anguish, and captivity." And he continues to comment:

> A person, then, because he is attached to prela-
> cies, or other such dignities . . . is considered
> and treated by God as a base slave and prisoner,
> not as a son . . . freedom cannot abide in a heart
> dominated by the appetites—in a slave's heart; it
> dwells in a liberated heart. . . .[26]

This critique is surely subdued and only in its beginnings, but it is there. The biblical images of darkness and the world are the equivalents of the corruption and evil which reigns in the world and society at large.

This sanjuanist pneumopathology, to paraphrase Voegelin, also moves beyond a symptomatology to the grounding source of evil and sin. And I would consider this to be a further aspect of the totalistic thrust of John's work. Here, I think, St. John joins up with the biblical tradition of the hardened heart as the source of evil, the heart closed to the Divine Summons. John also links up with the Greek Classic tradition and its tracing evil to *agnoia*, the closed self. As Voegelin put it, commenting on the Stoics:

> The Stoics . . . recognize mental disease as a dis-
> turbance of noetically ordered existence. The dis-
> ease affects both the passions and reason, but is
> caused neither by the one nor the other; it origi-
> nates in the questioning unrest, the *agnoia*, and
> in man's freedom to actualize the meaning of hu-
> manity potentially contained in the unrest or to
> botch the meaning.[27]

St. John himself will work through to a similar insight in varied ways. Early on in the *Ascent* he tries to distinguish symptom from root cause: "Since the things of the world cannot enter the soul, they are not in themselves an encumbrance or harm to it; rather, it is the will and appetite dwell-

ing within it that causes the damage."[28] This "disordered will"
I take to be a sanjuanist equivalent to the "closed self."

Later, in the *Night*, John will speak of the final purification as one which must extend to the soul's "very substance." The soul "feels terrible annihilation in its very substance and extreme poverty as though it were approaching
its end." Similarly he will say that the "darkness seems to
be substantial darkness, since it is felt in the deep substance
of the spirit."[29] This "substantial self" would seem to be the
sanjuanist equivalent of the self in its fundamental reality as
the source of the person's entire range of actualizations. This
is Voegelin's "questioning unrest," or the self in its aspect as
self-transcendent. The perversion of this funding source is
what must be critiqued, John wants to say. Should the purification not extend this far, one still remains "bound" and
so able to corrupt passions and reason again. I believe today
we might say that John is giving expression to the "systemic"
nature of human evil and sin. All manifestations of evil and
sin (the symptoms) are but expressions of the perverted self,
the self closed to and alienated from the Divine source of
love. John's special contribution here, I think, is to alert us
to how difficult it is to penetrate through to this deepest
level. If we follow John, a hermeneutics of suspicion will
derail into blindness unless it moves beyond a totalistic
symptomatology to the grounding source of the symptoms.
Reason, passions, Church, society, indeed the entire world,
all can be perverted by the perverted self. One of the great
contributions of John, I think, is to be sensitive to both
symptoms and cause, slighting neither one nor the other.

Let us dwell upon this last point a bit. I suspect that it
might be one of the more important sanjuanist correctives
in the current debate over a hermeneutics of suspicion. John
shares, I think correctly, the "bias" of the great tradition of
tracing the source of evil to the perverted self, rather than

to one or another individual or social symptom of evil. A perverted self can corrupt the best of realities if it remains perverted. Still, this does not lead John to slight or ignore symptomatology. In fact, the greater majority of the *Ascent-Night* is devoted to it. Why is that? John is aware of the dialectical interplay and mutual influence of symptoms and cause. The disoriented passions and beclouded thoughts of one's life, as well as the varied social pressures of one's society, are the realities which can contribute toward the self's perversion, habituating and blinding it. Of course, it works the other way too: the perverted self can further pollute all the passions, reasoning processes, and realities of Church and society. The point is this dialectic between symptoms and cause: neither should be slighted. The poem cited earlier from the *Ascent* I, 13, 11 (which John calls verses presented in *The Ascent of Mount Carmel*, from his drawing at the book's beginning) brings out this dialectical interplay quite succinctly. "To come to possess all desire the possession of nothing." Here the stress falls upon the symptoms: they must pass through the purification process. "And when you come to the possession of the all you must possess it without wanting anything."[30] Here the stress falls upon the "substantial" self's need for the purifying fires.

Thus, from the sanjuanist perspective, the confrontation with evil is more complex than many think. The rationalists, who think reason can solve all problems, are too naive for John, ignoring a whole range of realities that can be perverted: the passions, corrupting trends within Church and society, and the deeper source of the self-transcending self. Here John links up with the masters of suspicion of the second Enlightenment who trace the sources of iniquity to the passional (Freud, Nietzsche) and/or the social (Weber, Durkheim, Marx). But John would not be entirely happy with the second Enlightenment either, for he would see a need to move to the level of the soul's substance, that reality of the self as transcendentally open to the Divine: any blockage there needs to undergo the night. John happily and definitely stands with the Classic and Christian traditions on this point. Yet he does so in such a way that he doesn't slight the very real individual and social manifestations of human perversion. This sanjuanist balance is perhaps another manifestation of his completely open, self-critical, and totalistic orientation.[31]

Let me end by featuring a final characteristic of the sanjuanist pneumopathology which was suggested to me by my study of Eric Voegelin. In his own work on pathology, especially as he studied it in the Classic philosophers and the later Stoics, he noted that the Classic philosophers especially had

> . . . no term for "anxiety"; the tonality of being scared or frightened by a question to which no answer can be found is characteristically absent from the classic experience; the "scare" had to be introduced by the Stoics, as a pathological phenomenon, through the adjective *ptoiodes*. In the modern Western history of unrest, on the contrary, from the Hobbesian "fear of death" to Heidegger's *Angst,* the tonality has shifted from joyful participation in a theophany to the *agnoia ptoiodes,* to the hostile alienation from a reality that rather hides than reveals itself.[32]

Might I suggest that there is a similarly non-anxious "tonality" in the *Ascent-Night?* At this point I would reread the various stanzas of the poem (*The Dark Night*): in every one of them, despite their negations, there is this positive tonality of which Voegelin writes. Let me list these briefly:

stanza 1:   "Ah, the sheer grace!"

stanza 2:   "secure"
            "Ah, the sheer grace!"

stanza 3:   "that glad night"

stanza 4:   "This guided me
            More surely than the light of noon"

stanza 5:   "O guiding night!"
            "more lovely than the dawn!"

stanza 6:   "There in a breeze from the fanning
            cedars"

stanza 7:   "With His gentle hand,"

stanza 8:   "Leaving my cares
            Forgotten among the lilies."

Of course, it is this positive thrust which breaks out into song in John's *The Spiritual Canticle* and *The Living Flame of Love*.

Of course, the source of this "glad tonality" is the sanjuanist conviction of being supported by and embraced within a loving relationship to the Divine Bridegroom. Interestingly this does not land John in a dreamy utopianism, as we have seen. But, rather remarkably, it does not keep him from developing one of the most sustained treatments of pneumopathology in the Christian tradition. It is being "fired with love's urgent longings," as the great poem puts it, which seems to sensitize John to the varied manifestations/symptoms and final source of non-love. If you will, the attraction to a divine Lover seems to deepen and intensify John's awareness of evil and sin. Evil is not simply evil, but a closure to a loving relationship with the Divine. It is sin. John is convinced that as we fail to grow in our union with the divine Lover, we fall into varied corruptions of the passions, the thinking process, and our ecclesial and social structures. John's way of putting this, as we saw, was to argue that apart from God everything was evil. Perhaps we might say in our own terms that apart from a divine source of meaning and love, we fall into an increasingly frantic search for substitutes for love and meaning—namely, the passions, our own reason, ecclesial and social positions, etc. But none will ultimately satisfy (as John says, we are "fired with love's urgent longings"), and so we end up becoming the victim of our various fetishes.

"A more intense enkindling of another, better love (love of one's heavenly Bridegroom) is necessary for the vanquishing of the appetites," says John.[33] It is this Love which keeps us oriented in the direction of love. Without it, we become "inordinate," as John constantly puts it. Our task today, in the spirit of the sanjuanist critique, is to allow ourselves to be fired with love's urgent longings and to go and struggle against the varied ways in which we in our time and culture misorient (inordinate as a verb) our passions, our thinking, our churches, and our societies.[34]

Notes

[1]Cf. Gregory Baum, *Religion and Alienation*, p. 71, on this. Besides H. Stuart Hughes, *Consciousness and Society*, I would recommend the following as entries into the discussion of a hermeneutics of suspicion: Paul Ricoeur, "The Critique of Religion," in Charles E. Reagan and David Stewart, eds., *Paul Ricoeur: An Anthology of His Work* (Boston: Beacon, 1978), pp. 213–222, and his "Hermeneutics and the Critique of Ideology," in John B. Thompson, ed., *Hermeneutics and the Human Sciences*, pp. 63–100; John W. Van Den Hengel, *The Home of Meaning: The Her-*

meneutics of the Subject of Paul Ricoeur (Washington, D.C.: University Press of America, 1982), esp. pp. 203–208, is also helpful.

[2]Cf. V. H. Kooy, "Harden the Heart," in *The Interpreter's Dictionary of the Bible* 2 (Nashville: Abingdon, 1962), p. 524.

[3]St. Augustine, *City of God* XIV, 3 (David Knowles, ed. [Baltimore: Pelican, 1972], p. 551); cf. *Confessions* VIII, 5.

[4]There are enormously rich sources for a Christian pneumopathology here. As I suggested earlier, the rooting of the saints and mystics in praxis has a great deal to do with their subtle analyses of human iniquity. The entire discernment of spirits tradition is also a related phenomenon; cf. Keane, *Christian Ethics and Imagination*, pp. 39–41.

[5]The soteriological thrust of the non-Christian traditions is related to their refusal to separate theory and praxis. The highly therapeutic thrust of the classical inheritance is well brought out by Eric Voegelin in his varied works; cf. esp. *Order and History* I, *Israel and Revelation* (Baton Rouge, LA: Louisiana State University, 1956), esp. p. xiv: "The truth of order has to be gained and regained in the perpetual struggle against the fall from it; and the movement toward truth starts from a man's awareness of his existence in untruth. The diagnostic and therapeutic functions are inseparable in philosophy as a form of existence. And ever since Plato, in the disorder of his time, discovered the connection, philosophical inquiry has been one of the means of establishing islands of order in the disorder of the age."

[6]Cf. his *Anamnesis*, pp. 97–103 especially. Cf. also Eugene Webb, *Eric Voegelin: Philosopher of History* (Seattle: University of Washington, 1981), esp. pp. 193–207, for Voegelin's "mature" analysis of human iniquity, particularly through the diagnostic category of "gnosticism," which for Voegelin is a flight from reality into an illusionary dream world.

[7]*Ibid.*, p. 98.

[8]*Ibid.*, p. 99, referring mainly to *Tusculan Disputations* IV, 23–32.

[9]*Ibid.*, p. 100. The reader will note my use of the term "pneu-

mopathology" as coming from Voegelin's influence in this section
of his *Anamnesis*.

¹⁰The works of Ricoeur, Tracy, Baruzi, and Morel have been
particularly helpful to me in thinking through the literary aspects.
Egan, pp. 171–173, is also quite sensitive to this dimension of
John. Cf. his pp. 165–214 for an excellent introduction; then I
would suggest moving on into Baruzi and Morel. Von Balthasar,
The Glory of the Lord: A Theological Aesthetics (San Francisco:
Ignatius Press, 1986), 3, *Studies in Theological Style: Lay Styles*,
pp. 105–171, also offers a challenging interpretation, surfacing especially the aesthetic facets.

¹¹Morel, I, p. 219; cf. pp. 206–219 (my translation).

¹²On Niebuhr cf. Nathan A. Scott, Jr., ed., *The Legacy of
Reinhold Niebuhr* (Chicago: University of Chicago, 1975). I owe
the anecdotal comment to Robert McAfee Brown, *ibid.*, p. 3.

¹³*Ascent*, Prologue 8 (p. 72: all citations are from Kavanaugh
and Rodriguez, eds., *The Collected Works*) and I, 1, 1 (p. 73).

¹⁴*Ascent* III, 23, 1 (p. 252; cf. pp. 68–69 for the poem in its
entirety).

¹⁵*Ascent*, Prologue 3 (p. 70) and 9 (pp. 72–73); I, 2, 5 (p. 75);
I, 2, 1 (p. 75). It is in *The Living Flame of Love* 1, 14 that John
claims all are called to the mystical summit: cf. Egan, p. 202.

¹⁶*Ibid.*, pp. 102–104. Cf. Galilea, *The Future of Our Past*, p.
53.

¹⁷Cf. the studies of Baruzi, Morel, and Egan, pp. 165–214;
José C. Nieto, *Mystic, Rebel, Saint: A Study of St. John of the
Cross* (Geneva: Droz, 1979), is also helpful but I think too influenced by an "evangelistic" opposing of agape to caritas in his final
evaluation of John.

¹⁸*Ascent* I, 4, 4 (p. 79) and I, 11, 4 (p. 97).

¹⁹*Ascent* I, 11, 2 (p. 96).

²⁰Cf. p. 47 of Kavanaugh and Rodriguez; this is a helpful analysis of the sanjuanist anthropology. Cf. also Morel, *Le Sens de
l'existence selon S. Jean de la Croix*, II, *Logique*, pp. 25–30, on
the differences between John's and Aquinas' anthropology. The
chief issue is that John stresses not only intellect and will (like

Aquinas), but also memory. Is this related to John's sensitivity to the hidden, the forgotten, the "buried"?

[21]*Ascent* I, 9, 4 (p. 93).

[22]*Ascent* I, 1, 3 (p. 73) and I, 13, 1 (p. 101).

[23]*The Dark Night* II, 20, 5 (p. 377).

[24]*Ascent* II, 7, 11 (p. 125).

[25]*Ascent* III, 15, 2 (pp. 236–237).

[26]*Ascent* I, 4, 1 and 5–6 (pp. 78–80). Of course, there is no "modern" critical theory of social structures in John. That would seem to be primarily an insight of the late/second Enlightenment. The one "social structure" he could effectively deal with (the reform of Carmel) was his focus. Here we see an inchoate openness to social critique, I think.

[27]*Anamnesis,* p. 101.

[28]*Ascent* I, 3, 4 (p. 77).

[29]*The Dark Night* II, 6, 6 (p. 339) and II, 9, 3 (p. 347).

[30]Pp. 103–104.

[31]This "deepest, substantial self" (the biblical "heart") transcends individualism-privatism and classical socialism; that is, the self manifests itself on both an individual and social level, but can be reduced to neither.

[32]*Anamnesis,* p. 101.

[33]*Ascent* I, 14, 2 (p. 105).

[34]"Inordinate" appetites is the sanjuanist term for what we call today "misoriented" or "misdirected" tendencies: cf. esp. Book I of the *Ascent*. The question of the demonic/satanic in John's writings deserves special attention. My impression is that he simply accepts the "received" tradition and tends to stress the struggle against the diabolic in the later stages of the mystical ascent: cf., for example, *Ascent* II, 16, 3; II, 21, 8 and 12; II, 31, 2; III, 6, 2; III, 8, 3; *The Dark Night* I, 4, 3; II, 23 and 24. John probably would not accept the notion that the demonic is simply a symbolism for varied human experiences of evil, but would want to hypostatize the demonic. The fact that he tends to note the presence of the demonic at the later stages of the mystical journey is suggestive: is the satanic here a symbolism denoting the exceed-

ingly hidden and deceitful? Thus, the closer one moves to the
substantial self, the deeper becomes the evil which must be con-
fronted. One possible contemporary appropriation of the sanjuanist
demonology, then, might be to say that the satanic symbolizes the
dark, hidden reality of evil as a power which can radically disorient
the self away from the Divine: the anti-God tendency of the self;
evil as blasphemous idolatry, in other words. Cf. the suggestive
thoughts of Charles Davis, "The Inhumanity of Evil," in his *Body
as Spirit: The Nature of Religious Feeling* (New York: Seabury,
1976), pp. 109–124, and Langdon Gilkey, "The Human Predica-
ment: Estrangement and Sin," in his *Message and Existence: An
Introduction to Christian Theology* (New York: Seabury, 1979), pp.
111–157, esp. 147–150, the two best treatments of the satanic I
have seen.

VIII

Doing Christology with Saint Teresa of Avila

Teresa of Avila is of special interest to the christologian. For all Teresian scholars hold that she not only "assimilated" the standard christology of her time, but "had to" do christology in a fresh way. She made an innovative contribution to the forward march of the discipline of christology. In what follows I would like to try to surface her contribution in a somewhat sketchy way, and then suggest that she might serve as an important "christological midwife" as we approach one of the most delicate questions to confront christology in this late twentieth century. We are fortunate to possess a number of excellent studies of Teresa's christology which I would recommend to the reader. I would particularly single out Secundino Castro's *Cristologia Teresiana*, a careful and probing book-length study of her christology, which gathers together all the important Teresian texts and the secondary literature.[1]

Wherein lies Teresa's contribution? Some scholars say it is her accent upon the humanity of Jesus and her attempt to explore the role of Jesus' humanity in our Christian (spiritual) lives. Since she never seems to separate the humanity from the divinity of Jesus, I think it would be better to say that she accents the mediatorial role of Jesus in our spiritual lives. For *la Santa*, every aspect of our Christian lives is in some sense Jesus-mediated. On our way to God and our neighbor, we never really leave Jesus. That seems to be her fundamental intuition. Castro holds that, when it comes to

143

this issue, Teresa "feels herself able to make her doctrine known with authority. It is her favorite theme; her fundamental thesis."[2]

The capital sources for Teresa's teaching on our theme are *The Book of Her Life*, Chapter 22, and the Seventh Chapter of the Sixth Mansion of her *Interior Castle*. By this I mean that, although the mediatorial role of Jesus is a Teresian presupposition throughout all her writings, here at least the issue comes up for a more pointed, explicit treatment. Apparently it had become fashionable in some circles of religious and those pursuing the "contemplative life" to think that one must "surpass" the humanity of Jesus as one progresses up the "mystical ladder." The mysteries of the human Jesus were thought to be but stepping stones to his own ascent to the Father and glory. Likewise, prayer to and meditation upon these human mysteries were held to be but stepping stones for the contemplative beginner. *La Santa* puts it this way in the *Life:*

> In some books written on prayer it is said that even though the soul cannot reach this state of prayer by itself, since the work is an entirely supernatural one that the Lord effects in the soul, it will be able to help itself by lifting the spirit above all creatures and humbly raising it up, and that the soul can do this after having passed many years in the purgative life while it is advancing in the illuminative. . . . They give strong advice to rid oneself of all corporeal images and to approach contemplation of the Divinity. They say that in the case of those who are advancing, these corporeal images, even when referring to the humanity of Christ, are an obstacle or impediment to the most perfect contemplation. In sup-

port of this theory they quote what the Lord said
to the apostles about the coming of the Holy
Spirit—I mean at the time of his Ascension.
They think that since this work is entirely spiritual, any corporeal thing can hinder or impede it,
that one should try to think of God in a general
way, that He is everywhere, and that we are im-
mersed in Him.

This is good, it seems to me, sometimes; but
to withdraw completely from Christ or that this
divine Body be counted in a balance with our
own miseries or with all creation, I cannot endure.[3]

Teresian scholars debate just who it is that taught this
view of prayer in Teresa's time. The *alumbrados,* perhaps,
who seemed to stress a concept-less and image-less form of
prayer? Perhaps some spiritual writings popular in Teresa's
time were her target? In any case, we do know that there
was something of a struggle in contemplative circles over this
issue. For example, the fourteenth century theologian and
mystic Meister Eckhart seems to have recommended a kind
of "spiritualism" or moving beyond the corporeal, even Jesus'
humanity. In commenting upon John 16:7, in which the risen
Jesus says to his disciples "It is good for you that I go away,"
Eckhart states:

By that [Jesus] meant to speak not only to his
disciples of that time but to all who want to be
his disciples now and to follow him to higher perfection. His humanity is a hindrance to them in
the pleasure with which they depend on him. If
they are to follow God in all his ways, they must
not follow the ways of any human being, for
these will put them off the road to God.[4]

This "debate" on prayer is not simply an insular skirmish on an esoteric subject in ascetical theology. Prayer, that is, real prayer which has not grown routine and simply external, expresses in a concentrated manner the heart and center of a religion. It is, if you will, a microcosm of the nature of a particular religion. Thus, this struggle over the mediatorial role of Jesus in contemplative prayer is really a struggle over Jesus' mediatorial role in our Christian religion in general. Do we encounter God apart from Jesus? Do we receive the gift of salvation apart from Jesus? The spiritualist wants to say "Yes!" The real God—or the fullness of God—dwells in a region separated from something as human as Jesus. The real God is utterly "Transcendent" and beyond the finite. On a christological level we might conjecture that the Arian position is the "equivalent" to the spiritualist position. God could not become human, said the Arians,[5] because divine Transcendence cannot be "polluted" by human finitude. Likewise, the contemplative "spiritualist" wants to maintain that to really penetrate the Divine—to achieve mystical union—one must transcend the finite, even Jesus' finite humanity, and enter into a mystical conceptless and imageless rapture. Spiritualism possesses ecclesiological and sociological implications too. Its denigration of the human and finite and material fosters a simply other-worldly form of piety.

Now that the reader might be a bit more convinced of the centrality of the issue before us, let us pursue Teresa's exploration of the subject. As we proceed the reader should note how Teresa moves back and forth between her own experience and the heritage of the tradition. As I indicated earlier in this book, this "experiential" appropriation of the tradition is one of the major attractions of a "theological consultation" of the saints. "Many, many times I perceived . . . through experience," she tells us, that "if we are going to receive His great favors, we must do so through the most

sacred humanity of Christ, in whom God takes his delight."
And she finds this intuition confirmed in the experiences of
St. Paul and the other great saints:

> Once I had come to understand this truth, I
> carefully considered the lives of some of the
> saints, the great contemplatives, and found that
> they hadn't taken any other path: St. Francis
> demonstrates this through the stigmata; St. An-
> thony of Padua, with the Infant; St. Bernard
> found his delight in the Humanity; St. Catherine
> of Siena—and many others about whom your
> Reverence knows more than I.[6]

Let me try to summarize Teresa's views in four observations. First, in both the *Life* and *The Interior Castle* she
unambiguously teaches the mediatorial role of Jesus, human,
and of course divine, throughout the entirety of the Christian
life. There was no debate on Jesus' role as mediator for the
early stages of the spiritual ascent. But Teresa holds rather
emphatically that the human-divine Jesus remains our mediator even in the highest moments of mystical contemplation. The way of the most sacred humanity of Jesus, she tells
us in her *Life*, is the only path: "This Lord of ours is the
one through whom all things come to us." And so we "should
desire no other path even . . . at the summit of contemplation."[7] So, too, in *The Interior Castle:* speaking of those
about to enter the highest mystical states, she says,

> . . . if they lose the guide, who is the good Je-
> sus, they will not hit upon the right road. . . .
> The Lord Himself says that He is the way. . . .
> But let not those who can travel by the road of
> discursive thought condemn those who cannot, or
> judge them incapable of enjoying the sublime

blessings that lie enclosed in the mysteries of our good, Jesus Christ. Nor will anyone make me think, however spiritual he may be, that he will advance by trying to turn away from these mysteries.[8]

Secondly, Teresa advises us, given the role of Jesus in our experience, not to attempt to pass beyond the practice of prayer to the humanity of Jesus. According to her this can never be a hindrance in our Christian (spiritual) journey. "But that we should skillfully and carefully accustom ourselves to avoid striving with all our strength to keep this most sacred humanity always present (and please the Lord it would be present always), this, I say, is what I don't think is good," she asserts in the *Life*.[9] After all, she continues, an authentic mark of the spiritual life is the humility which comes from recognizing our dependence upon Jesus, like John at the foot of the cross. So, too, "we are not angels but we have a body,"[10] and so ordinarily it is through bodily supports (like meditation upon Jesus' humanity) that we flourish. These are the two supporting reasons she brings forward in the *Life*, but she concludes her discussion with an "afterthought" which sounds very much like the most basic argument of all:

> As often as we think of Christ we should recall the love with which He bestowed on us so many favors and what great love God showed us in giving us a pledge like this of His love, for love begets love.[11]

The Interior Castle seems to repeat this teaching: "To be always withdrawn from corporeal things and enkindled in love is the trait of angelic spirits, not of those who live in mortal bodies." As we need, then, prayer to the saints, "How much more is it necessary not to withdraw through one's own efforts from all our good and help which is the most sacred humanity of the Lord Jesus Christ."[12]

Thirdly, and probably most difficult, Teresa knows that there are times when meditation on Jesus' humanity will be suspended or "transcended" in a kind of wordless and imageless contemplation. This is the kind of prayer characteristic of the apophatic/negative mystical tradition, the way of (conceptless) unknowing. Let me indicate some of the more important Teresian texts on this matter: first, from the *Life:*

> This practice of turning aside from corporeal
> things must be good, certainly, since such spirit-
> ual persons advise it. But, in my opinion, the
> soul should be very advanced because until then
> it is clear that the Creator must be sought
> through creatures. Everything depends on the fa-
> vor the Lord grants to each soul. . . .
>
> When God desires to suspend all the faculties,
> as we have seen in the kinds of prayer that were
> mentioned, it is clear that, even though we may
> not so desire, this presence is taken away. Then
> let it be so—gladly; blessed be such a loss that
> enables us to enjoy more that which it seems is
> lost. For then the soul is occupied completely in
> loving the One whom the intellect labored to
> know, and loves what it didn't understand, and
> rejoices in so great a joy that it couldn't have ex-
> perienced it save by losing itself in order, as I
> say, to gain itself.[13]

Now, from *The Interior Castle*, where we encounter a somewhat more didactic presentation:

> By meditation I mean much discursive reflection
> with the intellect. . . .

> This prayer is the kind that those whom God
> has brought to supernatural things and to perfect
> contemplation are right in saying they cannot
> practice. As I have said, I don't know the reason,
> but usually they cannot practice discursive reflec-
> tion.[14]

It is at this point that we encounter one of the more difficult but crucial christological discoveries of Teresa. For, at first reading it would seem that Teresa is here contradicting her first point; namely, that Jesus is always our mediator, even in the moments of imageless contemplation. But that would be too simple a reading, for Teresa insists again that Jesus remains present. Even though we might not meditate upon Jesus' passion, she tells us in the *Life*, "who will prevent us from being with Him in His risen state?"[15] Here she seems to have in mind Jesus' presence in the Eucharist, for she immediately speaks of being able to gaze upon him in the Blessed Sacrament. But she goes on to argue that even when the mind withdraws from corporeal things, "the most sacred humanity of Christ must not be counted in a balance with other corporeal things."[16] Admittedly the language is confusing. Teresa seems to make new discoveries while she writes, something perhaps not untypical of narrative writings like the *Life*. But she seems to want to say that Jesus remains present in imageless contemplation; only the mode of that presence has changed. Do we remember her saying, when speaking of the loss of the discursively meditated upon presence of Jesus, ". . . blessed be such a loss that enables us to enjoy more that which it seems is lost"? The language in *The Interior Castle* seems clearer. We have already seen her say that those who cannot meditate discursively still enjoy the blessings of Jesus' humanity. But there are even clearer texts. Speaking of the one who has reached the summit of mystical perfection (being in the seventh dwelling place), she says that "such a person walks continually in an admirable way with Christ, our Lord, in whom the divine and the human are joined and who is always that person's companion."[17]

Jesus is always our mediator, but the mode of that mediation varies—this, I suggest, is the great Teresian discovery. Apparently in Teresa's experience there were times of enjoying Jesus' presence in both a kataphatic and an apophatic manner. The kataphatic manner—a more conceptual or imaged form of awareness of Jesus—was the more common. Many of the "visions"which Teresa enjoyed would perhaps come under this category too.[18] But she did know the apophatic presence of Jesus: wordless, imageless, "known" by "unknowing." "But let not those who can travel by the road of discursive thought condemn those who cannot, or judge them incapable of enjoying the sublime blessings that lie enclosed in the mysteries of our good, Jesus Christ."[19] From the way she explains her important "intellectual" vision of Jesus in the seventh mansions perhaps she has this non-conceptual (better: supraconceptual) presence of Jesus in mind: "The Lord appears in the center of the soul, not in an imaginative vision but in an intellectual one, although more delicate than those mentioned, as He appeared to the apostles without entering through the door when He said to them *pax vobis*."[20] This would help us understand her claim that "this intellectual vision of these three Persons [that is, the Trinity] and of the humanity of Christ always continues."[21]

Teresa does not present us with a fully developed "theory" of this important insight that Jesus' mediation takes either a "kataphatic" of an "apophatic" form. Or, expressed differently, Jesus' mediation is constant, but its mode varies. The narrative genre of both the *Life* and even *The Interior Castle* expresses the lived, existential quality of this mediation as one which alternates its mode in a flowing, back and forth, temporal manner. Perhaps this is one of the reasons why *la Santa* is attracted to the narrative genre: its flow of temporality expresses better the experiential-existential style of theology she practices. I also wouldn't want to discount her own feminist sensitivity as being one of the factors enabling her to develop her subtle christological distinctions. We have already noted, earlier in this book, her feminist imagery and even her *grito feminista* (feminist outrage) at the inferiorization of the women of her day. Clearly her experience as a woman is a mode through which she does spiritual theology and I venture to say christology. Does her own sensitivity to the womb experience help her to transcend simple sense experience (including discursive meditation, even on Jesus' humanity, together with various kinds of sensory visions and locutions) and to probe the "depths" of what is not outside and obvious, but more subtle, "within," or, better, "implicit" within our experience (supraconceptual aspects of experience, including that of Jesus' mediatorial presence)?[22]

I do wish that Teresa had tried to explain a bit more fully what a supraconceptual, apophatic experience of Jesus' presence might be. Both the apophatic tradition and the belief in the risen Jesus were solid aspects of Teresa's religio-cultural horizon. Our own contemporary emphasis upon an experiential retrieval of our tradition creates in us a yearning for more than Teresa seems to give. But before moving on, let me mention a few thoughts on this topic which are at least "suggested" by *la Madre*.

By holding that our access to God and to neighbor is always in some way a Jesus-mediated one, Teresa is at least implying that there is a "Jesus dimension" to the God-experience. Jesus in some way always qualifies this God-experience through whom we also reach our neighbor.[23] Of course, we may not always be conceptually aware of this Jesus-dimension, nor is that necessarily our ideal, given the high value which Teresa accords to an imageless and supraconceptual mode of prayer/contemplation. Still, irrespective of our "awareness," Jesus is "there." God's presence is always, for Teresa, Jesus' presence. Could we put this in another way, yet remaining faithful to Teresa? Might we say: God's presence is always a Jesus-like presence? Let us recall Teresa's comment: "As often as we think of Christ we should recall the love with which He bestowed on us so many favors and what great love God showed us in giving us a pledge like this of His love, for love begets love."[24] A Jesus-like experience is a love experience. Does this mean for Teresa that God's presence, precisely because it is always a Jesus-mediated presence, is always an experience of love: love begetting love?

Actually, Teresa speculates little about God's inner being. She looks more at her experience, at what she calls the "effects" of this Jesus-like God working within her: that the soul's "life in Christ is understood better, with the passing of time, by the effects this life has," she claims in *The Interior Castle*.[25] If you will, she infers something about the Divine Ground of her being from her experience of that Being in her life. And what is her experience (the "effects")?: "a forgetfulness of self," "a great desire to suffer" (as she powerfully puts it, "being able some way to help the Crucified"), striving for the virtues and practicing them (otherwise we will "always be dwarfs," she says), and service.[26] In other words, the Jesus-like quality of her experience leads her to believe in the Jesus-like quality of God.

Clearly we can deepen and intensify this Jesus-like experience of God and neighbor through meditation upon the mysteries of Jesus' sacred humanity. Teresa especially singles out the passion[27] where we learn the non-narcissistic nature of a Jesus-like love. But what about the imageless, supra-conceptual, apophatic experience of this Jesus-like God? Why this? Are there clues in Teresa on this issue? One possibility is the transcendent nature of the God-experience, even a Jesus-like God-experience. The Divine remains the more, the unbounded, the beyond whom words and images cannot fully express. Does the apophatic way bring this element of transcendence out? Teresa stresses our humility in the presence of this God who sometimes comes to us, not through our efforts at discursive meditation, but in a way suitable to the Divine's own wishes. Here is how she puts it in the *Life:*

> But the Lord desires us to recognize our uselessness and become like the little donkeys that turn the waterwheel . . . although their eyes are blinded and they don't know what they are doing, they obtain more water than the gardener does with all his activity.[28]

For Teresa the apophatic experience is like this: our "eyes are blinded" by the Divine who is greater than we are.

In the same place Teresa also stresses the properly Jesus-like quality of the apophatic way as a participation in the suffering Jesus: we should seek "consolation in trials for love of Him who always lived in the midst of them."[29] Thus, when God desires to act toward us as only God wishes we are learning something of that selfless love that characterized Jesus himself. The apophatic way perhaps brings out this Jesus-like aspect of purifying our ego, moving beyond all narcissism, including the possible narcissism of our concepts and images. The darkness of *apophasis* is a sharing in the darkness of Jesus' cross itself. In the Mother's strong words:

> Thus, with souls surrendered to His will . . . let

us always beseech God to grant us favors. Since
the soul receives permission to remain at the feet
of Christ, it should endeavor not to leave that
place . . . let it imitate the Magdalene, for if it is
strong, God will lead it into the desert.[30]

Looking back upon what we have seen in Teresa, then,
it appears that she does not simply reject the "spiritualist"
current in spirituality. She critically appropriates it. She presents us, not with an "either/or" but a "both/and." Let this
serve as our fourth observation on Teresa's christological
spirituality. What I mean is that she does not simply oppose
a Jesus-centeredness to the more spiritualist tradition of passing beyond even Jesus' humanity to the reality of God in
"naked unknowing and silence." Clearly she would have had
to do this were she to insist only upon a conceptual, imaged
mode of Jesus' mediation. Her important experiential contribution is to make the distinction between mediation and
mode-of-mediation. Our God-experience is always a Jesus-
mediated experience—here she sides with the tradition of
Jesus-centeredness, or what is sometimes called a "christocentric" form of theology and spirituality. But that Jesus-mediated God-experience can come to us in either the mode
of images/concepts, or in the more supraconceptual/image-
less mode of the apophatic way. By taking over this latter
mode Teresa appropriates the "spiritualist" current in spirituality, or what is sometimes called the late Hellenistic/Neo-
Platonic spiritual tradition.[31]

This christological insight is enormously liberating and
refreshingly balanced, I might add. As I indicated earlier,
by insisting upon the Jesus-mediated character of Christianity, Teresa frees herself from the "Arian" God of rigorous
and exaggerated transcendence who dwells only in *in*acces-
sible darkness. She also frees herself from a dualistic religion

which denigrates the concrete, material, institutional, and earthly. It is perhaps no accident that Teresa is known for her celebration of just these elements in her life and writings.[32] At the same time, by appropriating the apophatic tradition, she frees herself from an exaggerated "concrete-ism," if I may put it that way. Yes, the Divine Presence is always a Jesus-like presence. But that Presence can never be exhaustively "captured" in our concrete, conceptual or institutional expressions. This keeps us open to new forms of expression. This fosters a kind of critique of the conceptual and institutional, if I might put it that way. Hence, the marvelous balance and openness of Teresa's spiritual theology. We all feel that there's enough room for all of us in this kind of spirituality. We can all breathe in this kind of atmosphere!

I would like to suggest that we particularly need the guidance of Teresa today as we enter into the confrontation with and dialogue with the venerable non-Christian religions of the world. This new cross-cultural experience, which is being forced upon us by the new planetary experience of the globe—international communications media, political, social, cultural, and economic interdependency—is, I think, forcing the Christian to come to a new evaluation of the mediatorial role of Jesus himself. One cannot long be aware of a Buddha or the Hindu avatars without coming to question the unique position accorded Jesus by our Christian heritage. The reason why I recommend turning to the "midwifery" of St. Teresa is her attunement to Jesus—she is above all the "doctor of christocentrism"—and yet, simultaneously, her openness to integrating the Neo-Platonism of her day. She was a remarkably open and balanced woman. But she was also a Christian saint deeply in tune with Jesus and experientially aware of his salvific role in her life. As she could not contemplate a faith and piety which left Jesus behind in an effort to be open to the novel, so many of us cannot either.

Something of her attunement to Jesus is deeply needed by us as we venture forth in a sincere attempt to affirm what we can in the great non-Christian traditions. Secundino Castro, toward the end of his remarkable study of Teresa's christology, remarks that she "felt that her 'I' had become so transformed by Jesus Christ, that she began to understand the nature of anthropology in the light of christology."[33] For the Christian scholar I would recommend something like this as she or he ventures forth into the uncharted waters of the cross-cultural frontier. Our "I's" must become transformed into Jesus lest we lose our Christian substance in this new intercultural encounter.

Of course, *la Madre* does not have a theology of the religions. This is a question intensively posed by our experience more than by hers. At most we can speak of trying to formulate this kind of theology under her guidance; we can do theology in a Teresian kind of way. As her instincts led her to a "both/and" approach to the issue of christocentrism vs. Neo-Platonic supraconceptualism, so we can search for the both/and on our issue too. To allow such "open theological instincts" to take over would be the very least of the "Teresian" strategies we could employ. Allowing these "Teresian instincts" some room, then, what might be some Teresa-guided insights in this very delicate area of the theology of the religions?

So far as I can tell, two alternatives, which build upon the Teresian intuitions, offer themselves. The first, which seems less "radical" and seems to stay closer to Teresa's own explicit theological horizon, would be to suggest that the God-experience comes to us through the one mediation of Jesus, but this mediation takes place in multiple modes. Teresa, of course, knew of many modes of this Jesus-mediated presence of God. Listen to her words in *The Way of Perfection:*

> If contemplating, practicing mental and vocal
> prayer, taking care of the sick, helping with
> household chores, and working even at the lowli-
> est tasks are all ways of serving the Guest [that
> is, Jesus] who comes to be with us and eat and
> recreate, what difference does it make whether
> we serve in the one way or the other?[34]

This important text shows us the many modalities through which *la Santa* claimed to experience Jesus. Of course, for the most part we have stressed the two modes of discursive meditation upon the mysteries of Jesus' humanity and the supraconceptual way of "unknowing," since these were most under dispute in Teresa's experience. Still, despite Teresa's concentration upon these two "modes," she seems to have known of many.

In any case, a theology of the religions which would build upon this Teresian intuition of the God-experience as one which is only mediated through Jesus but comes to us in multiple modes would argue that the religious experiences of the non-Christian religions, when they are truly a God-experience, are various "modes" of that experience. Analo-gously with the supraconceptual mode, they are not experi-ences in the mode of explicit Jesus-categories. But they are God-experiences nonetheless, and Jesus is there, but in a mode different from his usual "Christian" form. As Teresa believed in the one God always mediated through Jesus but coming to us in multiple modes, so we might argue that the various non-Christian religions are different "modes" of this one God of Jesus Christ—at least insofar as these non-Chris-tian religions are genuinely open to this one God and in touch with it.

We might call this the thesis of the one mediator and

multiple modes of mediation. Here God is always and only the God of Jesus Christ, but in the mode or under the form of various "expressions," from explicitly Christian, to supra-conceptual, to possibly even non-Christian modes of expression. This, I think, is a genuinely "both/and" theology of the religions quite in keeping with the best Teresian intuitions. On the one hand we remain in tune with our Jesus-centered Christian substance. At the same time we open ourselves to the possible revelatory value of the non-Christian traditions. As we open ourselves to the non-Christian other, we don't find ourselves leaving Jesus behind, but finding him in a new mode. Again, let me repeat that I am not claiming that the above is Teresa's *explicit* view. I would only suggest that it is a possible implication of her very fruitful distinction between mediation and mode. Insofar as Teresa would seem to hold that the God-experience does not only come to us in the mode of explicit Jesus-categories, for the Divine transcends such categories, so perhaps the non-Christian religions might at times offer us varied modes of disclosure of this one God of Jesus Christ.

The more radical possibility, which seems correspondingly further removed from Teresa's own explicit theological horizon, would be to argue that not only do we have one mediator and multiple modes, but we also have multiple mediators. God is not *only* mediated through Jesus Christ. It is quite possible that the Buddha event, for example, represents a unique disclosure of the Divine in history distinct from the Jesus event. Or that the varied Hindu avatars, as a further example, do too. The Teresian-inspired condition would be to say that while God is *not only* mediated through Jesus, God is *always* mediated through him. For Teresa certainly affirms that every experience of God is a Jesus-experience too. Yet it is not so clear that it is only a Jesus-experience. This remains debatable. It seems to me that her acceptance of a God who transcends all categories can get along with either of our two possibilities.

This latter possibility, while admittedly somewhat radical and "distant" from Teresa's own explicit christology, deserves careful pondering. The "Teresian twist" to the theses of multiple mediators is to hold that Jesus may not be the only mediator of the God-experience, but he is always present in any mediation. There is never any God-experience apart from Jesus for Teresa. This enables us to affirm that the Jesus event remains always a dimension of God who acts salvifically on behalf of all. We need not and cannot surrender the salvific role of Jesus in our effort to affirm the other. Still, it may be that there is room in God for more than Jesus, and his saving work. And this may be "implied" in Teresa's acceptance of a God who transcends all categorizations, perhaps even the category of Jesus. Are the pressures of the cross-cultural interchange enabling us to discover implications in Teresa's acceptance of the apophatic tradition which even she didn't dream of?

At the very least, I would suggest that a Teresian-inspired theology of the religions rules out two possible extremes. On the one hand, there is a "closed" christocentrism which cannot accept the possibility of a God-experience transcending explicit Jesus categories. Teresa's experience seems to know of a christocentrism which can get along with multiple modalities of the one God of Jesus Christ. On the other hand, Teresa would have to reject any acceptance of the "other" which would demand surrendering the mediation of Jesus Christ. Openness to the other, yes. But only insofar as it is compatible with the mediatorial role of Jesus Christ. The more moderate thesis of "one mediator and multiple modes of mediation" clearly moves between these two extremes. It is a kind of "open" christocentrism. And the more radical thesis of both multiple mediators and multiple modes? Does this perhaps surrender too much of a Jesus-centrism in order to be open to the other? Or is it a valid implication of the Teresian christological presuppositions, now being surfaced under the pressure of our cross-cultural experience? Perhaps, in response to this, we can do no better than answer with the Mother's words. In the *Life*, at the end of her remarkable discussion of the role of Jesus' sacred humanity in the spiritual and contemplative life, she says:

> If your Reverence discusses with spiritual persons these things I have written on prayer, I again beg you that these persons be truly spiritual. For if they know only one road or have stalled in the middle, they will not be able to understand. . . . So experience and discretion are necessary in all matters. May the Lord in His goodness give them to us.[35]

An openness to the cross-cultural experience presupposes one willing to know more than "only one road." It demands courage, too; that is, not becoming "stalled in the middle." But at the same time, it demands the kind of spirituality and discretion that remains truly attuned to the substance of divine revelation.

Notes

[1]Secundino Castro, *Cristologia Teresiana* (Madrid: Editorial de Espiritualidad, 1978). Cf. also Enrique del Sagrado Corazon, "Doctrina y vivencia de Santa Teresa sobra el misterio de Cristo," *Revista de Espiritualidad* 22 (1963), 773–812; Tomas Alvaréz, "Jesucristo en la Experiencia de Santa Teresa," *Monte Carmelo* 88 (1980), 335–365; Antonio Moreno, "St. Teresa, Contemplation and the Humanity of Christ," *Review for Religious* 38 (1979), 912–923.

[2]*Ibid.*, p. 303. Helpful for this entire issue are Jean Dagens, "L'Humanité de Jésus," in his *Bérulle et les origines de la restauration catholique (1575–1611)* (Paris: Desclee de Brouwer, 1952), pp. 301–321, for the history of the issue. Bérulle, too, likewise took up this issue with great subtlety; see Dagens' work as well as Fernando Guillen Preckler, *Bérulle Aujourd'hui: Pour une spiritualité de l'humanité du Christ*. In English my own study might perhaps be found useful: "A Study of Bérulle's Christic Spirituality," in my *Jesus, Lord and Savior* (New York: Paulist, 1980), pp. 226–249. For speculative treatments of the theme see my *The Jesus Debate: A Survey and Synthesis* (New York: Paulist, 1985), pp. 299–323, and Karl Rahner, "The Eternal Significance of the Humanity of Jesus for Our Relationship with God," *Theological Investigations* III (Baltimore: Helicon, 1967), pp. 35–46.

[3]*Life* 22, 1 (p. 144).

[4]*Meister Eckhart: A Modern Translation*, Raymond Blackney, transl. (New York: Harper Torchbook, 1941), p. 199. For the possible targets of Teresa's attack, see Castro, p. 300.

[5]It is commonly held that Arius accepted a late Hellenistic view of God as finally so transcendent that becoming human was simply not thinkable.

[6]*Life* 22, 6 and 7 (p. 147); recall my earlier citation: ". . . there was nothing I understood until His Majesty gave me understanding through experience . . ." (22, 3 p. 145).

[7]*Life* 22, 7 (p. 147).

[8]*The Interior Castle* VI, 7, 6 (*The Collected Works of St. Teresa of Avila* II, Otilio Rodriguez and Kieran Kavanaugh, transls. [Washington, D.C.: Institute of Carmelite Studies, 1980], p. 400) and VI, 7, 12 (p. 403).

[9]*Life* 22, 9 (p. 147).

[10]*Life* 22, 10 (p. 148).

[11]*Life* 22, 14 (p. 150).

[12]*The Interior Castle* VI, 7, 6 (p. 399).

[13]*Life* 22, 8 and 9 (p. 147).

[14]*The Interior Castle* VI, 7, 7 (p. 400) and 11 (p. 402).

[15]*Life* 22, 6 (p. 146).

[16]*Life* 22, 8 (p. 147).

[17]*The Interior Castle* VI, 7, 9 (p. 401).

[18]See esp. the Seventh Mansion of *The Interior Castle*. Castro, pp. 50–70, offers an overview and interpretation of the Teresian christological visions and locutions.

[19]*The Interior Castle* VI, 7, 12 (p. 403).

[20]*The Interior Castle* VII, 2, 3 (p. 433). She speaks of a vision with an "inner eye" in VI, 9, 4 (p. 412).

[21]*Spiritual Testimonies* 65, 3 (*Collected Works* I, p. 364).

[22]Cf. our earlier comments on the feminist retrieval of St. Teresa: see the later part of chapter I.

[23]Teresa never separates the God-experience from the neighbor. To experience God is in some way to grow in love of the neighbor. Cf., for example, *The Interior Castle* VII, 4.

[24]See n. 11.

[25]*The Interior Castle* VII, 2, 6 (p. 435).

[26]*The Interior Castle* VII, 3, 2 (p. 438); VII, 3, 4 and 6 (p. 439); VII, 4, 9 (p. 447); and VII, 4, 12 (p. 448). Cf. Castro, pp. 145–231, where he surveys the christological quality of Teresa's ethical experience and teaching.

[27]Cf., for example, *The Interior Castle* VII, 4, 8. Cf. Castro, pp. 308–319.

[28]*Life* 22, 12 (p. 149).

[29]*Life* 22, 11 (p. 149).

[30]*Life* 22, 12 (p. 149).

[31]Sometimes also called an "abstract" spirituality vs. a more incarnational (Jesus-influenced) style of spirituality. See Dagens esp. in n. 2.

[32]Hence her great stress on locutions, visions, etc. See n. 18.

[33]Castro, p. 380 (my transl.).

[34]*The Way of Perfection* 17, 6 (*Collected Works* II, p. 101).

[35]*Life* 22, 18 (p. 151). For an "entry" into the cross-cultural problematic for christology, see my *The Jesus Debate*, pp. 39–42, 385–394, and Paul F. Knitter, *No Other Name?: A Critical Survey of Christian Attitudes Toward the World Religions* (Maryknoll, N.Y.: Orbis, 1985).

IX

Reflecting on Ministry with
St. Francis of Assisi
and St. Thérèse of Lisieux

H istory reveals that there always has been and likely always will be a struggle both over the meaning of ministerial governance and over who should actually be office-
holders within the Church. We see this reflected in the very
earliest strata of the New Testament, and it has remained a
continuous phenomenon in the history of the Church.[1] This
should not come as a surprise to us, given the extreme importance of ministerial governance or priesthood for the survival of the churches themselves. The "secular" analogue to
this is the intense struggle that goes on over who should
hold governing offices in society at large. Just as secular society grasps the enormous importance of governance for in-
suring that society's future, so the churches grasp the same.
One might rightly grasp the conclusion that societies/
churches not manifesting some kind of struggle over its office-holders are in some kind of "decay": perhaps massive
indifference on the part of the populace/faithful believers, or
a ruthless totalitarianism which crushes all possibility of external dissent. So I think we Church people—"governors,"
theologians, and people at large—ought to welcome a
healthy "struggle" over this very basic issue for our survival
itself. And those of us who are theologians ought to want to
participate in the great ministerial debates largely initiated
in our times by the likes of Karl Rahner, Raymond E. Brown,

Hans Urs von Balthasar, Hans Küng, Bernard Cooke, Thomas O'Meara, Langdon Gilkey, Rosemary Ruether, Jürgen Moltmann, Krister Stendahl, and others.[2]

What follows ought to be read as directed primarily to the issue of the priesthood (if we follow the terminology of the Roman Catholics, the Eastern Churches, and the Anglicans-Episcopalians), or to the chief ministry (if we follow the terminology of the Protestant traditions). Perhaps we could coin the title "ministerial governance" to cover both of the former, taking up a clue from Bernard Cooke's important contribution in this whole area.[3] To say that we are concerned with ministerial leadership is too vague, for all forms of ministry—whether the "chief" or priestly under consideration here, or the more particular and specialized kinds— are forms of leadership. "Ministerial governance" stresses the notion of a focal or chief kind of ministry in a community which holds final responsibility for that community's order. It is this which will be the object of our concern here, although one could rightly draw out implications for all forms of ministry and even for "secular" office-holders.

Typically I think it safe to suggest that ministerial governance finds itself struggling to avoid two grand extremes. On the one hand, there seems to be the perennial temptation of exploitativeness. That is, one uses one's office for one's own narcissistic and thus exploitative purposes. And, of course, this can occur on a more unconscious or hidden level, so that the office-holders either may not know that they are guilty of this on some levels of consciousness, or they may find various strategies to mask the fact from themselves. It might even be that the basic power structure of the society at large, within which the Church exists, is riddled through with a corrupt exploitativeness. This scenario makes it hard to believe that the Church's office-holders will escape the same kind of "lust for domination," to use the

traditional phrase so powerfully employed by Augustine.[4]
Down this path of exploitativeness lie all those horrible
"isms" so castigated by the great Protestant Reformers (in an
earlier time) and by many of the *patres* and *periti* of the
Second Vatican Council (in a more recent time): "hierarchi-
calism," "clericalism," elitism, etc. And many of us would
want to add misogynism, with its exclusion of women from
ministerial governance, to this list of exploitative horrors. If
the function of ministerial governance be that of preserving
the *ordo salutis*—the kind of order which truly nourishes
the salvation of the faithful—then exploitativeness twists this
order into a dreadful experience of oppression.

The other "grand extreme," of course, is anarchy in its
varied forms. Anarchy cripples the cohesiveness of the ecclesial community, thus making a true *ordo* or "order" im-
possible. Its forms are legion, but some of its more common
symptoms—a rampant individualism and relativism within
the churches, an immediate and basic distrust of ecclesial
authority (read: magisterium), a blatant scapegoating and vi-
lifying of office-holders, etc.—I wouldn't myself speak of "anticlericalism" as a form of anarchy: if clericalism be exploitativeness, then anticlericalism (at least in this sense) is a
virtuous imperative. Just as the first extreme can be unconscious or not so obvious to awareness, so can this one. It's
possible to live in an atmosphere permeated by anarchical
tendencies and to uncritically take these over into one's ecclesial posture and thinking. Sometimes just a plainly care-
less form of thinking can play into the hands of anarchy; for
example, the notion that the explosion of specialized ministries within the churches spells the extinction of the priesthood, as if the ecclesial *ordo* could possibly survive without
its ministry of governance.[5]

It would appear that these two grand extremes feed
upon one another. Exploitativeness likely breeds its coun-

terreaction in a rejection of the ecclesial *ordo* which, at the extreme, can derail into anarchy. And of course the reverse scenario is quite possible too. History seems to disclose both possibilities, one perhaps more dominant in a given epoch, then being overturned, followed by ecclesial equilibrium, then renewed tension and struggle, etc. A somewhat classical example of these two tendencies at war with one another is presented by the intense struggles for priestly reformation during the seventeenth century in France, for example: a highly corrupt hierarchy and priesthood in great decay, breeding great ecclesial indifference and disorder. The great reform work of Bérulle's Oratory, Olier's Sulpicians, the Eudists, the Vincentians, etc., can be seen as an attempt to transcend these extremes through the reformation of the priesthood.[6] What this would seem to teach us is that we must perpetually struggle to develop a form of ministerial governance or priesthood which fosters a truly saving or liberating form of order within the churches. An *ordo salutis* is quite different from totalitarianism: it is an expression of the new and alternative community of radical agape initiated by Jesus in history.[7]

This is the context in which I would like to set these brief reflections stimulated by St. Francis and St. Thérèse. We are consulting these saints with a kind of ministerial sensitivity, searching for their contribution to a "revisionist" form of ministerial governance along the lines proposed above. I would suggest that the *ordo* which truly liberates finds a kind of consummately lived expression in these two saints. That is, their lives are a lived expression of the kind of order ministerial governance should seek to nourish on the ecclesial, collective level. This is why they are apt sources worth consulting in our effort to revitalize the priesthood/ministerial governance today. They present us with a microcosm of the kind of liberating and saving order which should characterize the macrocosmic level of the Church itself. I particularly have in mind two rather "explosive" memories associated with these two great saints and mystics.

The reminiscence associated with St. Francis is found in most of the earlier lives of the mystic: Celano's *Second Life of St. Francis,* the *Legend of Perugia,* and the *Mirror of Perfection.* Let me quote from Celano's *Life:*

> While therefore the brothers were weeping very bitterly and grieving inconsolably [for Francis was dying], the holy father commanded that bread be brought to him. He *blessed and broke* it [Mt. 14.19] and gave a small piece of it to each one to eat. Commanding also that a book of the Gospels be brought, he asked that the Gospel according to St. John be read to him from the place that begins: *Before the feast of the Passover* [Jn. 13.1]. He was recalling that most holy supper which the Lord celebrated as his last supper with his disciples [Mt. 26.20–9; Mk. 14.17–25; Lk. 22.14–38]. He did all of this in reverent memory of that supper, showing thereby the deep love he had for his brothers.[8]

Now it is quite remarkable that in the context of the highly "cultic" and "clericalized" Church of Francis' day, he is remembered as proclaiming the words normally reserved to the ordained priest at the most "sacred" moment of the Eucharist, the consecration.

My own suggestion is that this must have been a quite explosive gesture. Given the reformist movements of Francis' time and the struggle over the unreformed clericalized episcopacy and priesthood of Francis' time, this volatile nature of Francis' act seems plausible. For remember: Francis was a "mere deacon," who probably would have preferred to remain unordained, if that would have allowed him the possibility of preaching. But again, in a clericalized Church, one had to be at least a deacon to preach. In any case, it is quite remarkable that St. Bonaventure's own later *Major Life of St. Francis,* when it retells this story of the end of Francis' life as found in the other lives, omits the reference to Francis' pronunciation of the eucharistic, consecratory words:

> When he had finished his inspiring admonition, he told them to bring a book of the Gospels and asked to have the passage of St. John read which begins, "Before the paschal feast began" (Jn. 13, 1). Then, as best he could, he intoned the psalm, "Loud is my cry to the Lord, the prayer I utter for the Lord's mercy," and recited it all down to the last verse, "Too long have honest hearts waited to see you grant me redress" (Ps. 141, 1–8).[9]

Did Bonaventure, himself a cardinal of the Holy Roman Church who strove mightily to tame extremist tendencies in the Franciscan tradition, grasp the explosive nature of this little "eucharistic" reminiscence as recorded in the other lives? Why else would he alter perhaps the most important part of this tradition?

I would suggest that we appropriate this great "Francis text" as a part of the continual struggle to create a form of ministerial governance which avoids the two grand extremes of oppressiveness on the one hand, and relativistic anarchy on the other. There is clearly no need to read the text as a denial of the legitimacy of the priesthood (or ministerial governance). That neither coheres with the text itself, nor does it make sense in terms of either the sensibilities of the tradition or our own contemporary experience. The text does, however, have a sting, and it seems particularly aimed at the temptation of priesthood to derail into an oppressive elitism or exclusivity. For by pronouncing the "most sacred consecratory words over the elements" which are reserved for the ordained priest and bishop Francis is presented in this text as disclosing a Church in which there are no elite, no special castes, no clericalized cadres. It is the revelation of a Church of "friars minor," people who are truly brothers (friars) because they renounce all pretense to special privilege or treatment (the *minores*). What we have here is a creative reappropriation of Mary's stinging *Magnificat:* "He has deposed the mighty from their thrones and raised the lowly to high places" (Lk 1:52). This Francis text subversively challenges any "throne theology," or "throne ministry."

This text, I think, summons us to a creative way of thinking about the priesthood or ministerial governance today, as well as to a creative ministerial praxis. Any ministerial governance that is truly governance possesses power, and, indeed, must and should possess power to be effective. The focal ministry holding final responsibility for the ecclesial order is indeed a powerful position. That is why it's worth struggling over. But Francis was in search of a form of power that was more evangelical, less possessive and oppressive. He wanted to eradicate egocentric clingingness from the Church, and a powerful way to do that is to cauterize such clingingness at the very center of ecclesial power. Could bishops and priests gladly welcome a gesture like Francis' today, in the conflictual atmosphere of our own Catholic Church as it struggles over the reformulation of its chief ministry? Could the chief ministers of the other churches gladly allow their people to say or perform whatever it is that is considered the most sacred preserve of their position? Such might be the test of the true nature of the *ordo* they are nourishing: either exploitative or truly evangelical and liberating. It would seem to me that the person who thinks this way of thinking denies the legitimacy and "uniqueness" of priesthood or ministerial governance has not yet appropriated the creative kind of ministerial insight flowing from Francis. Francis clearly contradicts a ministry of "thrones," it is true. I would suggest that one would have to hold such a "throne theology of ministry," either implicitly or explicitly, before he or she could grow upset at one I am suggesting here.

My second text comes, perhaps, from a somewhat more surprising source. For people commonly expect Francis to be somewhat upsetting: he was hard to domesticate, even for the powerful Roman Church itself! But Thérèse of Lisieux? Is she not the "little flower," soft and therefore unable to "bend" anything in a different direction? Yet readers persevering with this book up to now will recall the impressive feminist retrieval of this saint, and her powerful ecclesiology of love at a time when the Church had an ecclesiology of external structures and hierarchical castes. Perhaps it's not so surprising that we should find something quite challenging for our renewed theology of ministry in this *sainte?*

The text which I have in mind from Thérèse is actually a connected series of texts from her autobiography, *Story of a Soul*. The more I ponder this great work, the more convinced I become of its being a profound rethinking and reliving of all facets of ecclesiology. But let us allow the texts to speak for themselves.

> To be Your *Spouse*, to be a *Carmelite*, and by my union with You to be the *Mother* of souls, should not this suffice me? And yet it is not so. No doubt, these three privileges sum up my true *vocation: Carmelite, Spouse, Mother*, and yet I feel within me other *vocations*. I feel the *vocation* of the WARRIOR, THE PRIEST, THE APOSTLE,

THE DOCTOR, THE MARTYR. Finally, I feel
the need and desire of carrying out the most heroic deeds for *You, O Jesus*. I feel within my soul
the courage of the *Crusader,* the *Papal Guard,*
and I would want to die on the field of battle in
defense of the Church.[10]

This explosive text, from the famous Manuscript "B," has
usually been presented as a part of Thérèse's own struggle
to realize that, despite her being a cloistered nun, or rather
because of that fact, still she accomplishes in her own special
way what these vocations accomplish in theirs. Her ministry
of prayer and sacrifice is, on this view, the "heart" of the
Church which ultimately grounds the Church's work. As
Thérèse puts it in her later Manuscript "C," "No doubt it is
through prayer and sacrifice that we can help missionaries. . . ."[11] Pope Pius XI's declaration of Thérèse as principal
patronness of the missions in 1927, together with St. Francis
Xavier, is usually interpreted along these lines.

My own suggestion is that, while the above interpretation is true, it is not true enough. It tends to gloss over
the really challenging critique of ministry and Church found
in Thérèse's insight. It is true that Thérèse seems to con-
siderably tone down the potential explosiveness of her desire
to be a priest when she says, again in the Manuscript "B,"

I feel in me the *vocation of* the PRIEST. With
what love, O Jesus, I would carry You in my
hands when, at my voice, You would come down
from heaven. And with what love would I give
You to souls! But alas! while desiring to be a
Priest, I admire and envy the humility of St.
Francis of Assisi and I feel the *vocation* of imitat-
ing him in refusing the sublime dignity of the
Priesthood.[12]

Here she seems to surrender any desire for priesthood, contenting herself with her Carmelite ministry of prayer and sacrifice. And yet, one wonders. For she continues: "O Jesus, my Love, my Life, how can I combine these contrasts?"[13] She doesn't seem to give up her desire for priesthood, then. She feels called to it and even still more: "How can I realize the desires of my poor *little* soul?"[14] At last, some lines later, we arrive at her great insight:

> *Charity* gave me the key to my *vocation*. . . . I understood that the Church *had a Heart and that this Heart* was BURNING WITH LOVE. . . . I understood that LOVE COMPRISED ALL VOCATIONS, THAT LOVE WAS EVERYTHING. . . . MY VOCATION IS LOVE! . . . Thus I shall be everything, and thus my dream will be realized.[15]

My own suggestion would be that Thérèse is calling the church to rethink its definition of its various ministries, particularly that of priesthood—away from all tinge of exclusivity, and toward a ministry which nourishes love because it embodies an inclusivistic love. Such a ministry could even include women! Again, to return to the flow of our own narrative in this brief essay, Thérèse's text is a part of the great and ongoing struggle to develop a form of ministerial governance that transcends the extremes of exploitativeness and anarchy. Love/charity, of course, would be such: it preserves ecclesial order, but by including all. Again, no elitist castes. It seems to me that Thérèse is quite insistent upon this. She critiques not only the priesthood, but the doctors (theologians?), the apostles (the bishops, their "successors"?), even the Papal Guard (a symbol of positions "vehemently" reserved for males?). There is perhaps more of a critical "sting" in the Theresian charism than we have yet come to realize.

Her kinship with St. Francis, to whom she alludes, is perhaps much more subtle than we have hitherto thought. The way we understand priesthood/ministerial governance cannot remain the "same" after Thérèse, it seems to me.

I realize that the above might be too much for some admirers of Thérèse. But at times the saints are too much for us. As I put it earlier, they sometimes not only intensively live out the common understanding of the Church in their experience, but reveal the genuinely new, uncovering new dimensions of revelation not yet grasped. Perhaps the "sting" of the interpretation I have suggested it to be understood along these lines? This suggestion gains in plausibility, I think, when we recall some comments of Thérèse, already in her first Manuscript "A," comments stimulated by her visit to Rome before her entry into Carmel.

Something one first notices in Thérèse's travel narrative is the subtle critique of what I earlier called a "throne theology." Her reaction to the many nobility on her pilgrimage, for example, stimulates this outburst:

> Ah! far from dazzling us, all these titles and these *"de"* appeared to us as nothing but smoke.

> It is in heaven . . . that we shall know our titles of nobility. *Then shall every man have praise from God* [1 Cor. 4.5] and the one who on earth wanted to be the poorest, the most forgotten out of love of Jesus, will be the first, the *noblest*, and the richest![16]

She speaks also of priests, praising them for their goodness, but also claiming that while on this trip she realized that they are "weak and fragile men."[17] Does this illustrate her profound sensitivity to the ministry, her respect for it, and yet also her calling to reform it? For she claims that now she began to understand the "Reform of Carmel."[18]

But perhaps the most explosive outburst from her Roman pilgrimage comes toward the end of her account. Here she seems to be upset at the *exclusion* of women from varied churches, cloisters, and sanctuaries (?). And this brings forth from her what is, I think, a great dream of a more *inclusivistic* vision of Church and ministry. But let the reader judge for himself/herself, as he/she ponders this remarkable text:

> I still cannot understand why women are so easily excommunicated in Italy, for every minute someone was saying: "Don't enter here! Don't enter there, you will be excommunicated!" Ah! poor women, how they are misunderstood! And yet they love God in much larger numbers than men do and during the Passion of Our Lord, women had more courage than the apostles since they braved the insults of the soldiers and dared to dry the adorable Face of Jesus. It is undoubtedly because of this that He allows misunderstanding to be their lot on earth, since He chose it for Himself. In heaven, He will show that His thoughts are not men's thoughts, for then the *last will be first*.[19]

In placing all of these texts together, I am trying to suggest that they are connected. In fact, they seem so interconnected that I think we can plausibly speak of one great Theresian text on the rethinking and reliving of the Church and the ministry, and indeed of the Church's people at large. What seems to connect all of these texts is the critique of the throne theology, the caste system that creates a higher and a lower, a name with a *"de,"* as Thérèse so colorfully expresses it. To move from this toward a rethinking of the Jesus event and the Church in terms of charity or love must,

I think, bear upsetting implications for the Church's chief ministry of governance.

The subtle and gentle critique of the throne theology is what links Thérèse to St. Francis, I suggest. It is also what entitles us to place her among those struggling for a ministerial form of governance transcending exploitativeness and anarchy. At the same time, the gentle way in which Thérèse presents her critique, the "softness" of it, enables us to still name her the "little flower." She remains a "flower," for she is delicate, soft, and gentle. But she remains the "little" one, for like Francis' *minor* friars, she calls us to a Church and ministry in which the lowly are raised to high places.

Notes

[1]See now Edward Schillebeeckx, *The Church with a Human Face: A New and Expanded Theology of Ministry* (New York: Crossroad, 1985), which brings out something of the "struggle" involved.

[2]Fine bibliographies can be found in Bernard Cooke, *Ministry to Word and Sacraments: History and Theology* (Philadelphia: Fortress, 1980) and Thomas Franklin O'Meara, *Theology in Ministry*.

[3]See Cooke, pp. 187–214.

[4]Cf. *City of God* 1, 30, for example.

[5]O'Meara is particularly good on this point: cf. *passim*, but esp. pp. 134–175.

[6]See Michel Dupuy, *Se laisser à l'Esprit: l'itinéraire spirituel de Jean-Jacques Olier* (Paris: Cerf, 1982), esp. pp. 17–28, and *Bérulle et le sacerdoce* (Paris: P. Lethielleux, 1969).

[7]See my *The Jesus Debate*, esp. pp. 280–296, for this idea.

[8]*Celano's Second Life of St. Francis* 2, 217 (Marion A. Habig, ed., St. Francis of Assisi, *Writings and Early Biographies: English Omnibus of the Sources for the Life of St. Francis* [Chicago, Illinois: Franciscan Herald, 1973], p. 536). Cf. *Legend of Perugia* 117, and *Mirror of Perfection* 88.

[9]St. Bonaventure, *Major Life of St. Francis* I, XIV, 5 (*Writings*, p. 740).

[10]*Story of a Soul*, p. 192.

[11]*Ibid.*, p. 252.

[12]*Ibid.*, p. 192.

[13]*Ibid.*

[14]*Ibid.*

[15]*Ibid.*, p. 194.

[16]*Ibid.*, p. 121–122.

[17]*Ibid.*, p. 122.

[18]*Ibid.*

[19]*Ibid.*, p. 140.

X

Consulting "Everyday" Mystics

The reader will recall that we began our study of the place
of a consultation of the saints in theology with Thérèse
of Lisieux' somewhat lyrical statement on the "grandeur" of
the saints. Said she,

> I have always noticed that when I compared my-
> self to the saints, there is between them and me
> the same difference that exists between a moun-
> tain whose summit is lost in the clouds and the
> obscure grain of sand trampled underfoot by the
> passers-by.[1]

I cited this intriguing passage because I was trying to make
the case for our consultation of the saints. Obviously this
kind of theological consultation couldn't progress very far
were there not people of enormous depth of lived Christian
and religious experience worth consulting. St. Thérèse, I
felt, had captured something of this "depth of experience"
by her marvelous comparison. And something of her own
humility in the face of such grandeur would seem to be an
existential presupposition demanded of any theologian tred-
ding into these waters.

Still, there are dangers entailed in the above outlook
and emphasis. If you will, to pursue Thérèse's extended metaphor a bit, climbing a summit and getting lost in the clouds
can blind one to potential sources of richness or depth "down
below." This, of course, is one of the classical dangers entailed in concentrating only upon the canonized saints. While

I haven't done precisely that, I have concentrated upon the somewhat exceptional saints, mystics, or martyrs of the tradition. Particularly have I concentrated upon the "writing" mystics and saints, which is perhaps a typical bias of intellectuals and/or theologians. The danger in this kind of approach is that we will narrow our focus needlessly. After all, there are many people of enormous depths of religious and Christian experience "out there." They may not have the "recognition" or "status" of the people I've primarily focused upon up to this point, but they are "mystics" worth consulting nonetheless. In this regard, it's worth emphasizing that often the distinction between the "exceptionally recognized" mystic or saint and many of the rest of us is not a distinction in spiritual depth. Rather, it is often one of popular recognition and acknowledgment. I think St. Thérèse was on to this in her own way when she compared her own "way" to that of the "saints of grandeur" in the citation above. She spoke of her "little way": it did not soar above the clouds, but it was worth paying attention to nonetheless. As she put it,

> . . . God cannot inspire unrealizable desires. I can, then, in spite of my littleness, aspire to holiness. It is impossible for me to grow up, and so I must bear with myself such as I am with all my imperfections. But I want to seek out a means of going to heaven by a little way, a way that is very straight, very short, and totally new.[2]

As Joann Conn indicated in her study of St. Thérèse, the "little way" was perhaps a "totally new" way, as the saint phrases it, in the context of the spiritual theology of the times.[3] The clericalized and highly hierarchial Church of the times perhaps did tend to the same kind of elitism in its saints and mystics as it seemed to reinforce in its institutional organization. Thérèse seems to be a reaction against, or at least a balance to, this kind of stress upon the exceptional or highly acclaimed. But I fear that my book might also reinforce such a tendency. Hence the present chapter. It should be read as a balance to what has preceded it. This chapter is, if you will, the book's self-critique.[4]

To help us get our reflections started, I would like to turn to Karl Rahner's theology of "everyday things" as a kind of catalyst. I have borrowed the title of this chapter partly from Rahner, and when I think of a *theological* appreciation of the "everyday," I instinctively turn to him.[5] A glance at Rahner's multifaceted writings would reveal his always present fascination for the events and issues which emerge from our common human experience. And acquaintances and former students of his have appreciated this aspect of his personality and thought. Listen to what a former student and now a theologian, Robert Kress, has to say about this great theologian of our century:

> . . . Rahner is certainly a refutation of the suspicion that people so committed must be dull and distracted, withdrawn from and hostile to the joys of everyday life. During a 1979 visit to Louisville, Kentucky, Rahner was scheduled to visit a thoroughbred horse farm, the Oxmoor shopping center, and a church. Shortness of time forced a selection, so the church freely ceded to the shopping center. Department stores, especially their toy departments, have always fascinated Karl Rahner. On the following day, officially proclaimed "Karl Rahner Day in Louisville," he was promoted to the rank of Kentucky Colonel and Captain of the Belle of Louisville Riverboat, *honoris causa*. For him "Finding God in All Things"

is not only a principle of Ignatian mysticism but
is also an experience of daily life.[6]

Let me add to this that one of my more fascinating discoveries, when I was researching Karl Rahner in preparation for
my doctoral dissertation on his thought, was a "preface-in-
troduction" he wrote to a book on the songs of the Beatles![7]

Rahner's Jesuit formation, his love for and study of the
mysticism of St. Ignatius Loyola, and the thrust of the philosophical theology he slowly worked out in confrontation with
some of the great thinkers of modernity predisposed him to
develop an attunement to the "everyday." For him every
human being is a living attunement to a gracious Divine
Mystery which freely communicates itself with one and all.
As he put it in one of the titles of his works, we are "hearers
of the Word." Thus, in some sense we are all potentially
mystics. The mystical life is not an added on "extra" for the
human being, but the deepest calling of our being. I can still
remember the thrill I felt when I first read these words of
his, written in one of his meditative reflections on Ignatius'
Spiritual Exercises:

> When we have said everything about ourselves
> that is definable, then we have still really said
> nothing unless we have at least implicitly said
> that we are essentially turned toward the incom-
> prehensible God. This basic reference, which is
> therefore our very nature, is only understood if
> we freely let ourselves be seized by the incom-
> prehensible. The free acceptance or rejection of
> the mystery that we ourselves are as the poor
> reference to the mystery of fullness, constitutes
> our human existence. The pre-given object of our
> accepting or rejecting free decision is the mystery
> that we are; and this mystery is our nature, be-

cause the transcendence that we are and that we exercise brings together our existence and God's existence—and both of them as a mystery.[8]

Not only are we "potentially" mystics on the Rahnerian view. There was a glad optimism about Father Rahner (he died only March 30, 1984), whose theory of the "supernatural existential" led him to believe that we live in a graced universe in which not simply the possibility, but the reality, of transforming grace has entered. Thus, Jesus has really changed the quality of human history, initiating a process of divine self-communication and salvation. Thus, the Church can canonize saints, in recognition and celebration of the entrance of grace into history. Thus, too, "heaven" is a reality as the abode of the saved; "hell" remains a possibility only— a horrible possibility, it is true, but, for Rahner, still only a possibility. It is the triumph of grace which really fascinated Rahner—not the possibility of damnation.[9]

But Rahner was more optimistic yet. Not only has grace effectively entered history. Not only have some been transformed into saints and mystics, Jesus in a pleromatic and unique manner, and some others, primarily his mother Mary, in a kind of analogous way. Forces were at work which would probably even further increase the number of actual mystics in Christianity itself. The key study here is his often quoted "Christian Living Formerly and Today." People need to remember that Rahner was writing out of a West German, late twentieth century technological context. For him one of the great phenomena confronting Christianity was the demise of "Christendom," that historically conditioned fusion of Christian Church and "secular" state" which largely characterized "Christian" Europe through the Middle Ages and down into early modernity. As the state, at least as Rahner experienced it in West Germany, grew more "secularized," the modern Christian found herself/himself undergoing a somewhat transformed religious experience. The increasingly rationalized understanding of the forces of nature had "demythologized" God: people increasingly felt that it was no longer credible to think of God as a kind of superempirical object among other objects within the world, a way of thinking perhaps characteristic of former ages. This clearly turns the issue of God into a question, even for the one who wants to believe: "We live in an age in which the question is not so much how as sinners we may gain access to a gracious God who will justify us; on the contrary the impression is that it is God . . . who must justify himself to his creatures in their distress, while they for their part have no need of justification."[10]

Now it is this newly secularized culture for which the reality of God is becoming problematic which will force the emergence of a new kind of Christian, says Rahner. No longer simply "born" into a "folk-religion" whose mores and customs dominate the culture and dictate the laws and values, the individual Christian will have to arrive at his or her Christianity through an increasingly "personal experience" and "decision."[11] It is at this point in the article that Rahner expresses one of his more famous theological "predictions": ". . . the devout Christian of the future will either be a 'mystic', one who has 'experienced' something, or he will cease to be anything at all."[12] Here we have, I suggest, the Rahnerian optimism (which is different from utopianism, for it is based on the "Christian reality" of grace): not only are we *potentially* mystics, but our times will make of us who want to remain Christian true "mystics." Notice, too, how Rahner equates mysticism with experience: the mystic is the person of religious experience. To aid the believer he also suggests that we need to develop a "theology of mysticism" which will lead people to a discovery of the Divine within themselves, even though "many suppose that they could never discover such a thing in themselves." And he adds,

> The mystical approach of which we are speaking must impart the correct "image of God", based upon the accepted experience of man's basic orientation to God, the experience that the basis of man's existence is the abyss: that God is essentially the inconceivable; that his inconceivability grows, and yet does not derogate from the fact that the more rightly God is understood the more nearly does his self-bestowing love touch us. . . .[13]

These are beautiful and hopeful lines. The "average" and "everyday" person will discover and activate his or her mystic-making capacities. It seems to me that this became one of the perennial hinges of Rahnerian thought. In almost every piece he penned, the reader could usually count on some appeal to the "lived" mystical experience of the reader as the experiential basis to which Rahner would turn as a kind of "validation" of Christian beliefs. Rahner really believed in the "mystical" nature of our human experience, potentially and actually. His somewhat complicated "transcendental method" was basically an attempt to root Christian beliefs in the lived experiences (= mysticism) of everyday people. As if it were a kind of symbol of what I've been suggesting, Rahner's essay "All Saints" interprets this feast not simply as the ecclesial celebration of the elite who are canonized. It is also the feast of

> . . . the unknown saints as well, those who lived quietly in the land, the poor and the little ones who were great only in God's eyes, those who go unacclaimed in any of the rolls of honour belonging to the Church or to world history.[14]

Perhaps now the reader can understand why I instinctively turn to Karl Rahner when I think of "consulting" the everyday mystics.

Were I to be asked to recommend an essay of Rahner's which might succinctly and "explosively" transmit something of his appreciation for the mysticism of the unacclaimed, and the value of consulting them in precisely a theological manner, I would have to offer as my choice his essay "Everyday Things." Now we know where at least a part of this chapter's title came from. This little essay runs to approximately thirty pages in its English form, as if it were symbolizing even in its length the theological significance of the "little" and so the easily overlooked. The entire point of this essay is to bring home how the unacclaimed, precisely as unacclaimed, is loaded with theological significance. It is precisely because the ordinary and everyday is "ordinary" and "everyday" that it can become the "forum in which high-flown verbiage and bogus ideals are duly deflated, the chance to see things as they really are."[15] Perhaps our own concentration upon the appealing but still somewhat "elite" figures of our faith impedes us from "seeing things as they really are"? In any case, Rahner turns to the everyday with a packed power of elucidation in this essay. Here his mystical anthropology is put to work. He "instinctively" knows that it is in the common and everyday that the mystical experience of God is likely to be had, for "God is reached by acts that strip us of our selfishness, by care for others that makes us forget ourselves, by patience that engenders serenity and wisdom."[16]

Work, for example, the feature which characterizes for most of us our everyday, becomes for Rahner neither the most elated and noble nor the most depressing and deadening thing we do. Somewhere in between, it is usually just ordinary, repetitive, and basically tolerable. We often entertain high hopes for it, but soon enough it derails into the routine. Theologically, then, it seems to exemplify our "fallen state" and its need for the redemption of grace. It doesn't seem to be from anything "inherent" in work itself that we attain the ability to transcend the "tiresomeness, drabness, and (virtual) depersonalization of work."[17] Yet, we do so transcend all those things in a way which seems to point to the glad presence of a graced human world and existence.

Now that kind of theological probing of work, leading to an insight into the Christian doctrines of the fall and grace, is representative of Rahner's entire approach throughout this essay. "Getting about," again an enormously common and equally overlooked activity (unless we find ourselves somehow restricted), becomes through the Rahnerian lens a pointer to our pilgrimage-like form of existence as wanderers straddling a present which we hope will open out onto a more complete "future." It is another example of our human "transcendence" as referring us to a Beyond. The Acts call this "the way" (cf. Acts 9:2), for example. As if balancing all of this, the little essay on "sitting down" looks at another equally everyday activity of ours. Ultimately Rahner reads it as a sign that life's ultimate aim is to find meaning: we aren't simply restless wanderers. Sitting becomes a sacrament of our rootedness in a divine source of meaning. "He who conquers, I will grant him to sit with me on my throne" (Rev 3:21) is cited by Rahner at the essay's conclusion as a kind of biblical warrant for his thoughts.

Rahner's phenomenological ability to penetrate and expose the theological meaning of other everyday activities shines through on every page. G. K. Chesterton, I think, would highly appreciate the essay on laughter. "A good laugh is a sign of love; it may be said to give us a glimpse of, or a first lesson in, the love that God bears for every one of us."[18] Eating a meal, a somewhat less surprising subject for a eucharistic religion like Catholicism, symbolizes "the unity in which we long to merge ourselves."[19] Seeing and sleeping, another pair, also become glad experiences of grace. Both seem to presuppose a meaningful world: in seeing we gladly and soundly open ourselves to that meaning; the confidence which this kind of world arouses in us enables us to calmly surrender ourselves in sleep.

One can, of course, derive many lessons from this kind of theological consultation of our everyday mystical experience. For example, each of the above could be read as exemplifications of the Christian teaching on God as the ground and source of our own transcendental dynamism toward meaning and love. The banality of the everyday might be read as a pointer to the fragmentary nature of our this-worldly existence; the meaning and joy found in "sitting" and "eating," a foretaste of eternal life. Insights for the doctrine of eschatology, in other words, might be easily derived from this essay of Rahner's. So far as I can tell, Rahner chiefly chooses to set forth a more practical form of the doctrine of grace through these pages. The final essay is titled "On Grace in Everyday Life," and it reads as a kind of summary of the observations set forth earlier. If we look at it this way, we can say that at least one facet of this theological consultation of everyday mysticism is to aid us in finding out about the doctrine of grace. All of these essays illustrate, if you will, Rahner's thesis of the "supernatural existential": we live in a graced world. In some sense this little consultation of the everyday mystics not only illustrates a traditional teaching of our faith, it also serves as a kind of "corrective" to the late Baroque Catholic notion of a two-storied universe running along parallel tracts, one graced (= the supernatural) and one ungraced (= the natural). The very everydayness of grace breaks down any separate sphere of the purely natural or secular.[20]

God's grace cannot be found in the sense that
lost property is found. . . . It can only be found
in seeking God and surrendering ourselves to
him in self–abandoning love, unconditionally and
forever. We should continue to ask ourselves as
we go through life whether we feel that we are
being granted this favor of living by dying to ourselves.[21]

What I am suggesting at this point is that we follow Karl
Rahner's lead: perhaps he can teach us a *theological* sensitivity to the people and events of our everyday existence.
We really can learn theology from them! To return to the
categories employed in an earlier chapter, the unacclaimed
saint can serve both an appropriate and a critical function in
theology: the first, because he or she can experientially exemplify the tradition's own self-understanding; the second,
because he or she can develop or critique some facet of that
tradition for the sake of fidelity to the deepest meaning of
the tradition itself. Of course, I am speaking here primarily
to the theologian and the religious intellectual. I suspect that
many or perhaps even most of the non-doctored members
of the churches are already quite aware of what I am saying.

I suspect that many of us would find the claim plausible
that marriage is a "school of lived, everyday mysticism." Of
course, there are far too many failed marriages. And not all
married couples that "stick it out" achieve a profound depth
of mystical experience. All too often couples settle for a kind
of "détente," a living toleration of one another's "space." Still,
many of us know of the truly heroic married couples who
live out the basic virtues of the Christian life at a depth
which staggers the imagination of most of us. Here, if anywhere, one will find living examples of everyday mystics and
all too unacclaimed sanctity. Sometimes, too, one finds

something like a living martyrdom, if we would but loosen our imaginations a bit.

I have long felt that our academic theology has a lot to gain by a sustained and serious consultation of marital experience as it is found embodied in the heroic couples indicated in the above paragraph. The mystical tradition, of course, has a long tradition of turning to the nuptial experience for insights into the nature of the mystic's own union with the Divine Spouse. And ecclesiology has, at times, turned to marital experience as a possible image of the nature of the Church itself: the *ecclesia* (great Church) is found in concentrated fashion in the *ecclesiola* (the miniaturized Church of marriage). But perhaps we could learn a great deal by a more disciplined consultation of marriage? Systematic/speculative theology, for example, might want to regularly consult marriage as a source of insight into all the great themes of the tradition. I am convinced, even from my few years of marital experience, that the trained theological "phenomenologist" will find here in packed-concentrated form all the great mysteries.

Theological anthropology, pressing on a bit further now, might learn something about the human being as a mystery oriented toward relationships, from a consultation of marriage. The human as essentially relational and social finds here a kind of concentrated manifestation. The beauty and grandeur of "mystical" marriages serve as a critique of individualistic views of the human person. The somatic-sexual dimension of marriage might also "thicken" a relational anthropology, helping theologians to develop a more holistic, psychosomatic as well as relational vision of the human being. One of the great trends in Christian anthropology now is the recovery of the sociopolitical dimension of the human being. Does marital experience have its contribution to make here too? Is the marital/familial experience perhaps a con-

centrated symbol of the solidarity which society itself should
strive for? In this sense, is it also a critique of all tendencies
toward totalitarianism, all crushing of the kind of mutual regard and intimacy found in truly profound marriages?

Our theology of God, too, might learn a great deal from
the everyday mysticism of marriage. Here, if anywhere, we
find intensively expressed the varied modulations of the reality of love: love as joyful ecstasy, as grinding and painful
fidelity and openness to the other, as searing and costly cru-
cifixion and near-martyrdom, as playful fun and feasting, etc.
Is not this love, in all its forms, a rich source for an understanding of God as a reality of love? My own view is that
the theology of love, except for a few works, remains one of
the more undeveloped areas of contemporary theology. So
far as I can tell, there hasn't really been much *theological*
development in this area since Fénelon's great struggle over
the nature of "pure love." Perhaps a renewed attention to
marital mysticism from this perspective might introduce a
fresh infusion into the theology of love?[22] Related to this is
the traditional problem of theodicy too: how to reconcile the
reality of suffering with the reality of God? Here I have in
mind the fruitfulness of paying more attention to the therapeutic power of love in the marital relationship. Somehow
in deep marriages our wounds and sufferings undergo a kind
of healing transformation. Love seems to heal, yet without
violating our human integrity and independence. Is this a
possible model of how the Divine Love might heal and transform, yet without destroying our freedom?

Ecclesiology and sacramentology is perhaps the area
which attends most carefully to the marital experience, although apparently matters are still somewhat rudimentary
even here. The problem seems to be one of treating marriage
in a highly metaphorized (or spiritualized?) manner: it symbolizes the covenant between God and humanity found in

Church and sacraments, but in a somewhat esoteric way. The "love" between spouses and children, understood highly spiritualistically, symbolizes God's love in Church and sacraments. Were marital experience "consulted" in its more realistic and ample sense, one suspects that many implications would be felt in the areas of ecclesiology and sacramentology. Let me remind the reader, though, that I am speaking of the profoundly deep marriages of the unacclaimed "saints." But were these consulted, would our ecclesiologies and canon laws be less authoritarian and less sexist? Would our liturgies and rituals be more fun and playful? Would they be more rooted in the ordinary problems and concerns of our people? And clericalism: what would happen to that?[23]

And surely eschatology has a great deal to gain from a consultation of the marital experience. If, as Karl Rahner suggests, all theological eschatologies are futuristic extrapolations from our lived human and Christian experience, then surely marriage, particularly when it is lived at a "mystical depth," is a potent source waiting to be tapped. Spousal bliss and ecstasy in all its modes is perhaps a foretaste of what we mean by the bliss and ecstasy of heaven? The marital sense of the intertwinement of selves—as known to all spouses and parents of children—perhaps gives us a foretaste of what the communion of saints is all about. The purification of one's love through the marital experience—the unbelievable eradication of the narcissistic ego entailed—might perhaps give us some idea of what is symbolized by the doctrine of purgatory. Every married couple knows how it takes years for one's initial commitment to penetrate the very distinct levels of one's personality. The "purifying fires" of love slowly sink onto deeper and deeper levels. This distinction between initial commitment and gradual penetration—is that something of what is meant by purgatory? And the pain of separation and loss: is that a glimpse into the hell-experience?

A revisionist apokatastasis theory might also find in the marital experience some moorings. By apokatastasis I mean the belief that all will be saved. By revisionist, I mean a form of this theory which would be considered orthodox. Would the experience of the marital covenant, despite failure, be a kind of indication of God's covenanting with us, despite failure? To recall the comments of Von Balthasar cited earlier, does God's covenantal love not penetrate even our hell?

What about christology and soteriology? Surely these are mysteries of love in a preeminent sense: the breakthrough of a divinely unconditional love into human history through Jesus (= christology) acting to heal us of our lovelessness (= soteriology). In this sense, the kind of marital experience we are speaking about becomes a dramatic continuation of the Jesus event, and christologians would do well to dwell upon that experience for some of their insights. The hypostatic mystery of the union between God and humanity in Jesus might perhaps find a rather potent analogue in the union between spouses and children. Couples know that it is only the power of a divine and transcendent Love present in their union which gives them the ability to attain the heroic levels of selflessness demanded of all profound marriages. And related to christology is our trinitarian theology. This, too, just might receive a fresh reformulation in the light of a consultation of the marital experience. Is not the marital experience of finding life precisely through relationships something of what the trinitarian mystery is all about?

As we look back upon this little theological journey into marriage, we note one of the major suggestions of this book—namely, the mystics teach through exemplification, development, and correction. In some cases, a consultation of marital experience illustrates and experientially confirms dimensions of the Christian message. In others, it either "develops" the tradition (at least shows promise of doing so) or "corrects" inadequacies in the tradition's present self-under-standing. Even everyday mysticism can challenge the tra-dition and the theologians, as Rahner well knew. And I have only dealt with some of the more traditional areas of system-atics, a specialization in theology I feel most comfortable with. One wonders what moral theology might learn from a sustained consultation of such marital experience? For ex-ample, married couples of the depth I am referring to de-velop a kind of mutual attunement, enabling them to intuit each other's deepest needs and aspirations. Would this pro-vide us with an insight into what Karl Rahner calls the "moral instinct," the profound ability to discern moral good and evil, even in the most confusing of cases?[24] Does, as moralist Philip Keane suggests, the grandeur of such marriages in-dicate the basic intuition of the tradition that sexual expres-sion finds its best and most complete context within the mar-ital covenant?[25] Marriages of mystical depth are a kind of "moral magisterium," if we would but recall a phrase from Bernard Häring. They deserve a normal consultation by the moral theologian who particularly concentrates on ethical is-sues of immediate relevance to family life, it seems to me.

The above is only meant to be sketchy and suggestive, but perhaps I've made a somewhat plausible case for the fruitfulness of "consulting" the everyday mysticism found in our marital experiences. If you will, I've only tried to prolong Karl Rahner's analysis of everyday mysticism into the ex-perience of marriage which is such a common one for so many of us. There are, of course, many other candidates deserving of such a consultation, some of which I'll try to mention here. As a Roman Catholic, I spontaneously think of the unsung, unacclaimed parish priests I have known who seem to live out their ministry at an extraordinary depth of intensity. And, thankfully, I've been blessed with acquaint-ances in the Episcopal, Protestant, and Eastern Orthodox

priesthood/ministry of similar depth. I also think of the depth
of mystical experience found among the "contemplatives" of
our ecclesial traditions, ranging from Trappist priests, Carmelite nuns, Orthodox monks and nuns, Anglican and Lutheran monks and nuns, to more experimental forms of contemplation found in widely diverse locales. Surely here
something of Rahner's "testing of bogus ideals" is to be encountered? In our era of easily being dazzled by the novel
and spectacular, it would be a horrible blindness to the presence of God's transforming grace to ignore the grandeur and
beauty shining out from these many great but unacclaimed
saints.

Were the reader to push me, wanting me to develop a
bit more fully the theological lessons to be learned from
these last-mentioned, I would offer the following, but only
as a catalyst for further thought. The first group—the unsung
priests and ministers—particularly bring out for me the mysterious reality pointed to in the biblical notion of *kenosis*.
By this I mean they help us discover and value the reality
of an unflashy and rather selfless service—self-emptying—
on behalf of others. The fact that it is so often unsung and
unacclaimed seems to be a dimension of kenosis. This kind
of "servitude," to use the language of the French school of
spirituality, doesn't push itself, doesn't thrust itself upon
others. It works for others, but non-intrusively and non-vi-
olently. I believe this is the deepest meaning behind the
notion of *anéantissement*, so favored in the French spiritual
tradition. In this way, these "curates" are a rich source for
a revitalized appreciation of the importance of the theme of
kenosis in all areas of theology. By theologically listening to
them, the theologian might learn something of the kenotic
dimension, not only of the ministry and the Church, but
even of a God who communicates the divine presence in the
kenosis of the incarnation itself. I would not want to argue

that this first group might not exemplify other dimensions of our Christian existence. I am only suggesting that the possibility and credibility of kenosis as a true fulfillment of our humanity shines out in them in a kind of magnified way.

Our second group—the "contemplatives" of all types—surface another reality which, curiously, was also very beloved to the French spiritual tradition. I am thinking now of what mystics like Bérulle and Olier called "adoration," that profound sense of awe in the presence of the Incomprehensible Mystery which we call God. Perhaps today we might also call this the virtue of "reverence." Surely there is a need for a revitalized sense of reverence. Reverence and violence simply do not mix. I find it hard to believe that one could really revere a human being and then torture him or her. And could one really revere the earth, and then turn around and abuse it? And could one really be said to revere one's wife and children, and then batter them? Reverence is the dazzlement that the glow of grace arouses in our being. It seems to me that people who truly embody this grand virtue are also supremely unnoticed. The adorer focuses, not upon the self, but upon the others and the Other with a sense of enrapturing marvel. It somehow goes along quite congenially with the mystic-monk and nun, whether in "older" or in "experimental" form. The true contemplatives I have been graced with knowing—I am thinking fondly now of a Trappist monk, my Carmelite sisters-friends, and two other women—have about them, I have come to believe, a kind of "glow." It is, I think, a facet of the radiance they experience in their moments of profound adoration and reverence—a kind of after-glow, as it were. I can only liken it to the wonder a child displays upon experiencing something wonderful for the first time. In a child it often comes from innocence and perhaps even naiveté. In these, my contemplative friends, I at first thought I was seeing this kind of childish naiveté. I've since come to believe it's rather this after-glow. They deeply know something of what Gerard Manley Hopkins called "the dearest freshness deep down things."[26]

In the "modernistic" and reductionistic atmosphere of his times, Baron Friedrich von Hügel knew the importance of the virtue of adoration. The human ability and need to adore was, for him, an indication of the inadequacy of philosophies and theologies which ignored the Transcendent More. ". . . if prayer, and especially adoration, are the soul of religion, then the firm ontological stance which forms the basis for such prayer and adoration must likewise pertain to the very soul of religion," said the baron.[27] Perhaps there is something of this same reductionism in our own late twentieth century atmosphere in the industrialized west? Perhaps a consultation of our contemplative friends might enable us to surface in a renewed way the transcendental factor in all the great mysteries of our faith? In God, surely, but also the glow of the transcendent as it manifests itself in world, society, and Church.

And now it is time to return to the "everyday."

Notes

[1]*Story of a Soul*, p. 207.
[2]*Ibid.*
[3]See Conn's already cited study, "Thérèse of Lisieux from a Feminist Perspective."
[4]Here I would particularly like to thank my colleague, Professor George Worgul, for suggesting and urging that I write a chapter like this one for this book.
[5]See Egan, pp. 373–374; John Carmody, "The Realism of Christian Life," in Leo J. O'Donovan, ed., *A World of Grace: An*

Introduction to the Themes and Foundations of Karl Rahner's Theology (New York: Seabury, 1980), pp. 138–152; and *The Von Balthasar Reader*, esp. p. 342: ". . . for Christians the highest value is not the experience of transcendence but persevering through the grayness of everyday in faith, hope, and love."

⁶Robert Kress, *A Rahner Handbook* (Atlanta: John Knox, 1982), pp. 6–7.

⁷"*Vorwort*," in Georg Geppert, *Songs der Beatles: Texte und Interpretation*, Scriften zur Katechetik, Paul Neuenzeit, ed., Vol. XI (München: Kösel, 1968), pp. 7–9.

⁸*Spiritual Exercises* (New York: Herder and Herder, 1965), pp. 100–101.

⁹See *Foundations of Christian Faith*, p. 435.

¹⁰In *Theological Investigations* VII (New York: Herder and Herder, 1971), pp. 3–24 at 12.

¹¹*Ibid.*, p. 15.

¹²*Ibid.*

¹³*Ibid.*

¹⁴"All Saints," *Theological Investigations* VIII, pp. 24–29 at 26.

¹⁵"Everyday Things," in *Belief Today* (New York: Sheed and Ward, 1967), pp. 13–43 at 14.

¹⁶*Ibid.*, p. 15.

¹⁷*Ibid.*, p. 19.

¹⁸*Ibid.*, p. 30; cf. G. K. Chesterton, *Orthodoxy* (Garden City, N.Y.: Image, 1959), p. 160: "There was some one thing that was too great for God to show us when He walked upon the earth; and I have sometimes fancied that it was His mirth."

¹⁹*Ibid.*, p. 34.

²⁰Karl Rahner, "Concerning the Relationship between Nature and Grace," *Theological Investigations* I (Baltimore: Helicon, 1961), pp. 297–317, esp. p. 315: ". . . man can experiment with himself only in the region of God's supernatural loving will, he can never find the nature he wants in a 'chemically pure' state separated from its supernatural existential. Nature in this sense continues to be a remainder concept, but a necessary and objectively justified one, if one wishes to achieve reflexive consciousness of

that unexactedness of grace which goes together with man's inner, unconditional ordination to it."

[21]"Everyday Things," p. 43.

[22]Interestingly, Rahner is one of the handful of theologians to dwell upon the theme of love in a sustained, theological way. Cf., for example, his "The 'Commandment' of Love in Relation to the Other Commandments," in *Theological Investigations* V (Baltimore: Helicon, 1966), pp. 439–459. Three very helpful works on love: C. S. Lewis, *The Four Loves* (New York: Harcourt Brace Jovanovich, 1960); Hans Urs von Balthasar, *Love Alone* (New York: Herder and Herder, 1969); and Daniel Day Williams, *The Spirit and the Forms of Love* (New York: Harper and Row, 1968).

[23]See Bernard Cooke, *Sacraments and Sacramentality* (Mystic, CT: Twenty-Third Publications, 1983), for a sustained consultation of marriage with the purpose of developing a theology of Church and sacraments.

[24]On Rahner's notion of the "moral instinct of faith," see, for example, his "The Problem of Genetic Manipulation," *Theological Investigations* IX (New York: Seabury, 1972), pp. 225–252 at 238–243.

[25]See his *Christian Ethics and Imagination*, pp. 120–121.

[26]From his celebrated poem, "God's Grandeur." For the French school, see Louis Cognet, *Post-Reformation Spirituality* (New York: Hawthorn, 1959), pp. 56–115.

[27]Translated from "Petite consultation sur les difficultés concernant Dieu," by Joseph P. Whelan, *The Spirituality of Friedrich von Hügel*, p. 80.

Indexes